PROJECT AIR FORCE

The tanKer Aerial Refueling Model for Analysis (KARMA)

Dahlia Anne Goldfeld, Richard Mason

Prepared for the United States Air Force

For more information on this publication, visit www.rand.org/t/RR2682

Library of Congress Cataloging-in-Publication Data is available for this publication.
ISBN: 978-1-9774-0150-2

Published by the RAND Corporation, Santa Monica, Calif.
© Copyright 2019 RAND Corporation
RAND® is a registered trademark.

Support RAND
Make a tax-deductible charitable contribution at
www.rand.org/giving/contribute

www.rand.org

Preface

Over the past few years, the U.S. Department of Defense and U.S. Air Force have become increasingly concerned with countering an anti-access/area denial (A2/AD) strategy. The U.S. military as a global power must typically project power over long distances and operate from forward bases. Aerial refueling is a critical capability enabling Air Force power projection and forward employment operations. Denying access and basing is likely to be a critical component of a potential adversary's strategy wishing to disrupt U.S. power projection.

The research reported here was commissioned by the Air Force Air Mobility Command, Strategic Plans and Programs (AF AMC/A5/8), and conducted within the Force Modernization and Employment Program of RAND Project AIR FORCE as part of a fiscal year 2017 core funded project, Tankers and Airlift in Future Anti-Access/Area Denial Environments, to evaluate the capability of the Mobility Air Forces (MAF) to support combat operations in an A2/AD environment in the 2030 time frame. The main focus was on aerially refueling tankers. As part of this work, we developed a model, tanKer Air Refueling Model for Analysis (KARMA), to evaluate tanker operations in detail and assess the capability of the fleet to support required combat sorties. The main purpose of this report is to record the algorithmic details of KARMA and explain the inputs and outputs of the model. This report will be of use to anyone who wishes to use KARMA to assess sortie generation capabilities in a war scenario where resources may be limited because of diminished aerial refueling capacity or air base attack. We hope that it will be of particular use to planners, operators, and analysts at Air Mobility Command who are involved with tanker operations.

Two companion reports were also produced during this project. The first presents the results of our analysis evaluating the capability of the MAF to support operations in an A2/AD environment (David T. Orletsky, Michael Kennedy, Bradley DeBlois, Daniel M. Norton, Richard Mason, Dahlia Anne Goldfeld, Andrew Karode, Jeff Hagen, James S. Chow, James Williams, Alexander C. Hou, and Michael J. Lostumbo, *Options to Enhance Air Mobility in Anti-Access/Area Denial Environments*, Santa Monica, Calif.: RAND Corporation, forthcoming, not available to the general public). That report evaluates the expected operations in the 2030 time frame and suggests and evaluates approaches to enhance operations. A second report focuses on air survivability tankers and presents an assessment of the tanker vulnerability while in flight (Jeff Hagen, Bradley DeBlois, James S. Chow, Alexander C. Hou, Fred Timson, and James Williams, *Assessing Survivability Options for Air Refueling Tankers*, Santa Monica, Calif.: RAND Corporation, forthcoming, not available to the general public).

RAND Project AIR FORCE

RAND Project AIR FORCE (PAF), a division of the RAND Corporation, is the U.S. Air Force's federally funded research and development center for studies and analyses. PAF provides the Air Force with independent analyses of policy alternatives affecting the development, employment, combat readiness, and support of current and future air, space, and cyber forces. Research is conducted in four programs: Strategy and Doctrine; Force Modernization and Employment; Manpower, Personnel, and Training; and Resource Management. The research reported here was prepared under contract FA7014-16-D-1000.

Additional information about PAF is available on our website: www.rand.org/paf.

This report documents work originally shared with the U.S. Air Force on October 6, 2017. The draft report, issued on October 26, 2017, was reviewed by formal peer reviewers and U.S. Air Force subject-matter experts.

Contents

Figures

Tables

Summary

Over the past few years, the U.S. Department of Defense and U.S. Air Force (USAF) have become increasingly concerned with countering an anti-access/area denial (A2/AD) strategy. The U.S. military as a global power must typically project power over long distances and operate from forward bases. Aerial refueling is a critical capability enabling USAF power projection and forward employment operations. Denying access and basing is likely to be a critical component of a potential adversary's strategy wishing to disrupt U.S. power projection.

The tanKer Air Refueling Model for Analysis (KARMA) was developed as part of a RAND Project AIR FORCE project, sponsored by the Air Force Air Mobility Command, Strategic Plans and Programs (AF AMC/A5/8), to evaluate the capability of the tanker fleet to support combat operations in an A2/AD environment. KARMA enables an analyst to simulate the extent to which a tanker force can aerially refuel the combat aircraft in a denied environment. The primary assessment metric likely to be used is the sortie generation rate of all or particular aircraft types over any period of simulated time. The USAF Synthetic Theater Operations Research Model was used to generate the air tasking order (ATO) for the combat aircraft in a scenario and was used as an input to KARMA. The RAND Combat Operations in Denied Environments Theater Air Base Vulnerability Assessment Model was used to provide an estimate of air base damage as a result of missile attack and was also an input to KARMA. KARMA is a flexible, fast-running model, allowing users to explore a variety of scenarios, basing structures, concepts of operations, enemy attack patterns, and tanker aircraft capabilities.

Questions that can be addressed by KARMA include the following:

- Under various scenarios, will U.S. air operations be constrained by tanker capacity, including both (1) offload capacity and (2) the number of booms and drogues available?
- How resilient will tanker operations be to Red attacks on Blue bases? How do the results of air base attacks on both tanker and receiver operations interact in determining the success of overall U.S. air operations?
- How do these answers depend on basing options for tanker aircraft and for receiver aircraft?
- How do these answers depend on both tanker and receiver tactics and procedures?

Overview of KARMA

KARMA is a deterministic model written in Python 2.7. It simulates the ability of the United States and its allies (Blue) to generate airpower over the course of a conflict scenario, given a desired ATO, aircraft laydowns, and resource limitations. KARMA includes a detailed model of tanker operations, allocating individual tankers to individual refueling requests at specific times and tanker orbits.

Scenario parameters include a Blue ATO that contains information about all non-tanker sorties over the course of a period of a war.[1] Additional scenario parameters are tanker orbit locations, aircraft beddown, and air base information, which includes key resource availability and degradations of resources due to missile attacks or other causes. Aircraft mission parameters include the type of aircraft, the type of mission flown, target location, time on target, munitions package and configuration carried, fuel reserve, and the minimum and maximum allowable separation (distance) between an aircraft's final tanker orbit and the aircraft's ultimate destination. Aircraft in KARMA have associated data files that contain performance information, such as fuel capacity limits, airspeeds, and fuel-burn rates. There is also a file that contains a list of munitions and their respective weights and another file that contains a library of munitions configurations.

Varying these parameters allows one to gauge their respective effects on Blue's resiliency in a conflict, generally reflected by sortie generation capabilities. KARMA produces many outputs codified in various output files. These files include an amended version of the input ATO, detailing which of the planned sorties flew and which were scrubbed and why, and a tanker ATO, detailing what tankers flew at what times and from which bases and which refueling requests they served. The main steps in KARMA are visualized in Figures S.1 and S.2. Constraints on the outlined steps in Figure S.1 are in red. Figure S.2 summarizes the main blocks of KARMA with a focus on time sequence.

---

[1] An ATO typically covers a 24- to 72-hour period. When we refer to *ATO*, we mean a flying schedule over the course of a user-defined scenario that essentially strings together a sequence of ATOs over time.

Figure S.1. The Main Steps of KARMA

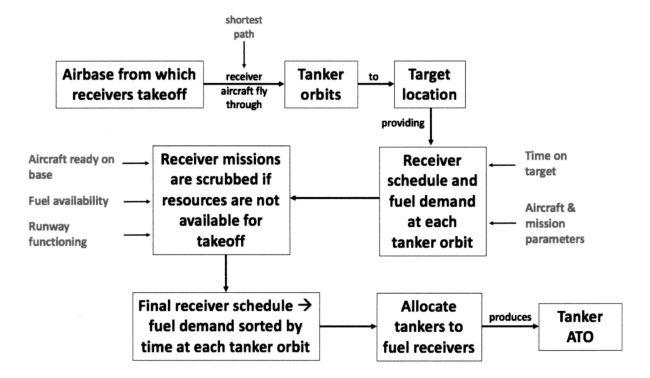

Figure S.2. The Main Steps of KARMA over Time

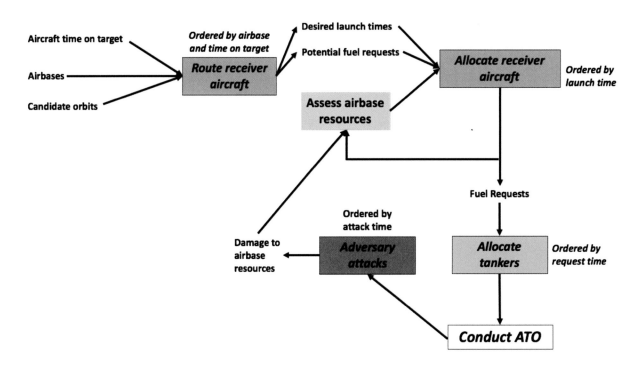

Each combat sortie has a target destination and time on target specified in the ATO. From a set of possible tanker rendezvous locations,[2] KARMA finds the path with the minimum number of feasible journey legs and refueling stops that allows the sortie to reach its target; from the fixed time on target, the entire flight schedule of the sortie is calculated. The feasibility of receiver takeoff times is then checked to verify that there is enough fuel on base, that there is a long-enough runway available for takeoff, and that there are enough suitable aircraft of the correct mission design system available (not in flight and not being maintained). Any receiver sorties that cannot take off are scrubbed. This yields a final receiver schedule, and receiver fuel requests at each orbit are sorted by time.

A tanker schedule is then calculated based on the receiver fuel requests at each orbit. A tanker is allocated to refuel the earliest still-unmet receiver refueling request in the following way. First, KARMA evaluates whether any tanker already at the same orbit as the receiver can satisfy the request. If there are no on-orbit tankers that can fulfill the request, KARMA searches for a tanker at an air base that is available and can provide enough fuel to fulfill the request. If one is available, it is scheduled to fly to the orbit and fulfill the request. If no single tanker on the ground can fulfill the request, then combinations of tankers on orbit or on the ground and on orbit that can fulfill the request are searched for, and, if such a combination exists, it is used to fulfill the request. When a tanker is first flown to an orbit to fulfill a request, KARMA checks whether the same tanker can entirely fulfill future requests at the same orbit, and then the tanker fulfills those requests. If there are no other future requests to which the tanker could contribute, then it returns to base; if the tanker might partially contribute to future requests, then it stays on orbit with its time of return to base not yet determined.

If there is no tanker or combination of tankers that can fulfill a receiver request, then the receiver mission is scrubbed. This forces previous tanker commitments that were made to the now-scrubbed receiver mission to be undone. Because the flight schedules of those tankers are partly undone, any other tankers and receivers that were scheduled to interact with those tankers may also have their schedules partly undone, possibly placing some entries back into the list of unrefueled receiver requests. In this way, tankers are allocated until all receiver requests have either been met or scrubbed and a feasible tanker schedule has been produced.[3]

---

[2] The set of possible rendezvous locations is a user input. The model will fail to find a plan for receiver aircraft for which there are insufficient rendezvous location options. The user is alerted of this fact and can add an additional tanker orbit to fix the problem. The algorithm by which the feasibility of rendezvous locations is determined is described in great detail later in the report.

[3] Air base attacks affect air base resources, including tankers. If KARMA is being used to evaluate a scenario's sortie potential and tanking viability with air base attacks, the number of receivers that are able to take off likely goes down, as does the number of tankers. The algorithm to allocate tankers given an air base attack is slightly more complex and is addressed in the main body of this report.

Acknowledgments

The authors and project team are grateful for the support that we received throughout this research effort from the project's sponsors at Air Mobility Command (AMC), initially Maj Gen Jon Thomas and later Maj Gen John Wood. The project's action officers and staff at AMC Strategic Plans and Programs (A5/8) and Studies, Analysis and Assessments (A9) were critical to the success of this effort and provided much useful information and many insights into tanker operations and challenges. Craig Lundy and Bryan Riba in AMC Future Concepts (A5/8XC) and Jim Donovan in the AMC Directorate of Studies and Analysis (A9A) were always gracious hosts at Scott Air Force Base and handled our many inquiries with speed and thoroughness. This project and report are much improved thanks to their assistance. We also thank John O'Neill and Pete Szabo of AMC A9 and David Merrill of Booz Allen Hamilton for insightful comments on the work and for providing data.

We are very grateful to Charlie Carson at Boeing for providing performance data and other required information on the KC-46.

At Air Force Materiel Command, we would like to thank Lee Ann Rutledge and Vince Raska, both at the Air Force Research Laboratory Aerospace Systems Directorate, Aerospace Vehicles Technology Assessment and Simulation Branch (AFRL/RQQD), and Gary Tarka at the Air Force Life Cycle Management Center Aeronautical Systems Development Division (AFLCMC/XZA), who provided a great deal of information early in the project about ongoing work on the topic.

The responsibility for any errors lies with the authors.

Abbreviations

A2/AD	anti-access/area denial
ABAT	Air Base Attack Tool
AMC	Air Mobility Command
ARCEM	Air Refueling Combat Employment Model
ATO	air tasking order
C2	command and control
CAP	combat air patrol
CFPS	Combat Flight Planning Software
CODE	Combat Operations in Denied Environments
CONOPS	concept of operations
CSV	comma-separated value
JASSM	Joint Air-to-Surface Standoff Missile
JASSM-ER	Joint Air-to-Surface Standoff Missile–Extended Range
KARMA	tanKer Air Refueling Model for Analysis
MAF	Mobility Air Forces
MDS	mission design system
nmi	nautical mile
PAF	RAND Project AIR FORCE
STORM	Synthetic Theater Operations Research Model
TAB-VAM	Theater Air Base Vulnerability Assessment Model
USAF	U.S. Air Force
USN	U.S. Navy

1. Introduction

Over the past few years, the U.S. Department of Defense and U.S. Air Force (USAF) have become increasingly concerned with countering an anti-access/area denial (A2/AD) strategy. The U.S. military as a global power must typically project power over long distances and operate from forward bases. Aerial refueling is a critical capability enabling USAF power projection and forward employment operations. Denying access and basing is likely to be a critical component of a potential adversary's strategy wishing to disrupt U.S. power projection.

In fiscal year 2017, RAND Project AIR FORCE conducted a project, sponsored by the Air Force Air Mobility Command, Strategic Plans and Programs (AF AMC/A5/8), to evaluate the capability of the Mobility Air Forces (MAF) to support combat operations in an A2/AD environment in the 2030 time frame. The main focus was on air refueling tankers. As part of this work, we developed a model, tanKer Air Refueling Model for Analysis (KARMA), to evaluate tanker operations in detail and assess the capability of the tanker fleet to support required combat sorties. The details of this model are presented in this report.

KARMA enables an analyst to simulate the extent to which a tanker force can aerially refuel the combat aircraft in permissive or denied environments. KARMA is a flexible, fast-running model, allowing users to explore a variety of scenarios, basing structures, concepts of operations (CONOPSs), enemy attack patterns, and tanker aircraft capabilities. It was designed to be higher fidelity than some other combat models in order to assess the likely effect of new technologies and tactics[4] on USAF's ability to provide tanker support to the combat air fleet. KARMA represents a major advance in tanker modeling at RAND.[5] In this application, we used the USAF Synthetic Theater Operations Research Model (STORM) to generate an air tasking order (ATO) for the combat aircraft in a scenario as an input to KARMA. We drew extensively on the RAND Combat Operations in Denied Environments (CODE) family of models to provide expected levels of air base damage given specific ballistic and cruise missile attacks.

Two companion reports were also produced during this project. The first presents the results of our analysis evaluating the capability of the MAF to support operations in an A2/AD environment (Orletsky et al., forthcoming). We evaluated the expected operations in the 2030 time frame to suggest approaches to enhance operations. A second report focuses on air

---

[4] For example, one might be interested in how a fleet of very large tankers or a CONOP such as buddy tanking would affect receiver sortie generation.

[5] A few representative research reports on past RAND work on operations in A2/AD environments are Emerson, 1982; Stillion and Orletsky, 1999; Stevens, Ochmanek, and Schwartz, 2007; Lostumbo et al., 2013; Romano et al., 2016; and Tripp et al., 2015.

survivability and presents the results of our assessment of the tanker vulnerability (Hagen et al., forthcoming).

KARMA Features

KARMA explicitly represents the characteristics of the three important tanker aircraft that may be in the USAF tanker fleet in the 2030 time frame, the KC-135R/T, KC-10,[6] and KC-46A. It includes explicit representation of whether receiver aircraft require boom or drogue refueling and the different capabilities of the tanker aircraft in these areas. Both the KC-46A and the KC-10 are equipped with both a flying boom and a center-mounted hose-and-drogue system.[7] This means that they can refuel receivers requiring either kind of refueling on the same mission. The KC-135 can do one or the other, but not both, on a single mission. The KC-46A, some KC-10s, and some KC-135s can also be configured so that they can refuel two aircraft from two different drogues simultaneously. The drogues are deployed from two pods, one mounted under each wing. The system is called the multipoint refueling system on the KC-135 and wing aerial refueling pods on the KC-10. The KC-46A, KC-10, and some KC-135s can also themselves be refueled in the air by another tanker. KARMA can incorporate new tanker designs of any kind.

KARMA was also designed to evaluate the efficacy of different tanker and receiver CONOPSs that could potentially make it more difficult for an adversary to block U.S. operations. These CONOPSs generally involve employing dynamic changes in aircraft basing to protect aircraft. Variations include adaptive basing, dispersed basing, flex basing, and maneuver basing. The basic idea behind these CONOPSs is that forces are moved around to complicate enemy targeting or to protect aircraft and other critical resources by placing them outside of key threat rings. These CONOPSs can harness additional resiliency measures, including active defenses, passive defenses, camouflage, concealment, deception, and left-of-launch operations.[8]

Any of these CONOPSs could have a large effect on the efficacy of the tanker force. For example, if the combat air force has to travel significantly farther than it would otherwise, it has a correspondingly greater aerial refueling requirement. Furthermore, operating locations needed to execute these CONOPSs may be austere or not originally designed to be major operating bases. Moving large numbers of aircraft to these bases would thus strain runway capacities, fuel and munitions storage and resupply, and maintenance. This could decrease the inherent efficiency of receiver and tanker aircraft, further challenging overall operational capabilities.

---

[6] Note that Air Mobility Command (AMC) has concluded that the KC-10 fleet is being phased out.

[7] Since the 1950s, USAF has used a flying boom system for aerial refueling of its fixed-wing aircraft because large aircraft, such as bombers, benefit from the higher fuel-flow rates that can be delivered via a flying boom. However, U.S. Navy (USN) aircraft, U.S. Marine Corps aircraft, and foreign national aircraft still use hose-and-drogue systems (Bolkom, 2006).

[8] Left-of-launch operations aim to neutralize or destroy adversary missiles before they are launched.

Modeling Tanker Operations

Other air war models, such as STORM and the Theater Air Base Vulnerability Assessment Model (TAB-VAM), have, to date, treated air refueling operations at a lower level of fidelity, tending only to assume that enough tanker missions are flown to deliver approximately as much fuel as the combat air force requires but not tracking which tanker aircraft interacts with which receiver aircraft.[9] Our intent was that KARMA would simulate tanker operations more faithfully while still being able to leverage those other models' strengths: i.e., using schedules of combat sorties developed in STORM and base attack outcomes modeled in TAB-VAM.

At the other end of the spectrum, AMC has detailed air refueling planning tools, such as the Air Refueling Combat Employment Model (ARCEM) (Jackson, 2009). ARCEM is described as a "powerful" but "time consuming" tool, and the "difficulty of using" it has inspired several proposals for different quick-look tools (Hackler, 2008). AMC analysts advised us that very substantial effort would be required to incorporate a hypothetical new tanker or radical new concept into ARCEM, but RAND researchers might wish to quickly explore many such concepts. KARMA, therefore, is intended to be a useful intermediate tool: simple enough to quickly explore new scenarios but detailed enough to accurately capture the effects of those scenarios on tanker operations.

KARMA is a greedy algorithm that attempts to find a feasible tanker ATO and does not guarantee that the solution is globally optimal in its consumption of resources. Barnes et al. (2004) point out that finding the optimal refueling schedule is a complex problem and, even with some simplifying assumptions, is comparable to planning problems known to be extremely challenging computationally.[10]

Panos (2007) proposes a method for scheduling refueling operations using approximate dynamic programming. This method has the advantage over KARMA that it should converge to an optimal solution within its assumptions. However, KARMA has two notable advantages over the Panos method:

1. KARMA has a more realistic model of aircraft fuel usage, especially including the fact that airspeed and fuel burn may vary with the weight of the aircraft, so that a fully fueled tanker burns fuel more rapidly than a lightly loaded one. The Panos method makes the simplifying assumption that aircraft fuel burn is constant (which in turn makes the optimization problem easier).

2. KARMA should find a feasible schedule significantly faster (perhaps 100 times faster) than the Panos method converges to a schedule that is optimal, assuming linear fuel burn.

---

[9] For discussion of STORM, see Seymour, 2014, and Bickel, 2014. For discussion of TAB-VAM, see Thomas et al., 2015.

[10] For the technically minded reader, it is a non-deterministic polynomial-time hard problem.

McCoy (2010), on the other hand, proposes a relatively detailed model of fuel consumption over the course of a flight, in order to plan single-tanker–single-receiver aerial refueling sorties but did not attempt more-complicated scheduling or the generation of a tanker ATO. KARMA has a similar level of physics fidelity but allows for complex missions with multiple refueling interactions and generates an entire tanker ATO.

As a war scenario progresses, some Blue assets (runways, aircraft, fuel storage) may be destroyed by Red attacks, forcing Blue to change plans. At the same time, some Blue aircraft may already be in the air, in accordance with the old plan. KARMA will then formulate a new plan that reflects the new situation in the air and on the ground. An advantage of the flexibility and relatively fast run time of KARMA is that it can rapidly model Blue's ability to replan and adapt to combat events and show how Blue's planning changes over the course of a war.

A representative set of questions that are well addressed by KARMA include the following:

- Under various scenarios, will U.S. air operations be constrained by tanker capacity, including both (1) offload capacity and (2) the number of booms and drogues available?
- How resilient will tanker operations be to Red attacks on Blue bases? How do attack impacts on both tanker and receiver operations interact in determining the success of overall U.S. air operations?
- How do the answers depend on basing options for tanker aircraft and for receiver aircraft?
- How do the answers depend on both tanker and receiver refueling tactics and procedures?

Overview of KARMA

KARMA is a deterministic model written in Python 2.7. It simulates the ability of the United States and its allies (Blue) to generate airpower over the course of a conflict scenario, given aircraft laydown and resource limitations. It is event-stepped in time. KARMA includes a detailed model of tanker operations, allocating individual tankers to individual refueling requests at specific times and tanker orbits.

Scenario parameters include an original Blue ATO that includes information about all non-tanker sorties. Additional scenario parameters are tanker orbit locations, aircraft beddown, and air base information, which includes key resource availability and degradations of resources due to missile attacks or other causes. Aircraft mission parameters include the type of mission flown, target location, time on target, munitions package and configuration carried, fuel reserve, and the minimum and maximum allowable separation between an aircraft's final tanker orbit and the aircraft's ultimate destination. Aircraft in KARMA have associated data files that contain performance information, such as fuel capacity limits, airspeeds, and fuel-burn rates by altitude and weight. There is also a file that contains a list of munitions and their respective weights, and another file that is essentially a lookup table of munitions configurations. These input files are described in Appendix A.

A feature of KARMA is that it can accept aircraft descriptions at different levels of fidelity, depending on what data are available. In general, the desired aircraft speed and resulting fuel-burn rate in a given flight mode are functions of the aircraft's instantaneous total weight, depending on the amount of fuel and munitions or other payload the aircraft is currently carrying. KARMA can accept a long list of data points with the appropriate speed and fuel-burn rate at many possible aircraft weights and, therefore, can produce a highly accurate calculation of the aircraft's speed and fuel burn over the course of its mission. On the other hand, KARMA can also accept a more approximate curve with only a few data points. In the extreme case, the data file could contain only a single data point, with the aircraft's speed and fuel-burn rate at a single weight; KARMA would then use that single constant speed and fuel-burn rate for the aircraft under all circumstances.

Similarly, the rate at which an aircraft's fuel tank can accept fuel can be a function of how much fuel is already in the tank. If that information is available, KARMA can accept a detailed curve of fuel-onload rate as a function of current fuel amount and thus do high-accuracy nonlinear modeling of the necessary refueling time in different circumstances. On the other hand, if detailed information is not available, aircraft can also be characterized by a single constant fuel-onload rate.

As yet another example, each aircraft type has a constant minimum runway length for takeoff, but, if the data are available, the maximum takeoff weight as a function of runway length and airport altitude and temperature can be specified in detail. KARMA can use these more detailed data to allow tanker aircraft to take off with reduced fuel loads from short runways or hot air bases. Again, the intent is for KARMA to be flexible with regard to how much aircraft performance data are available to the model.

Varying input parameters allows their respective effects on Blue's resiliency in a conflict to be gauged. KARMA produces many outputs codified in various output files. These files include an amended version of the input ATO, detailing which of the planned sorties flew and which were scrubbed and why, and a tanker ATO, detailing what tankers flew at what times and from which bases and which refueling requests they served. The main steps in KARMA are visualized in Figures 1.1 and 1.2. KARMA steps that require user input are color-coded to match the files from which the data are sourced. Constraints on KARMA steps are represented by data that are fed in through the narrow purple arrows. The text that follows accompanies these figures and summarizes these main steps. Full details can be found later in the report.

Figure 1.1. Receiver Scheduling

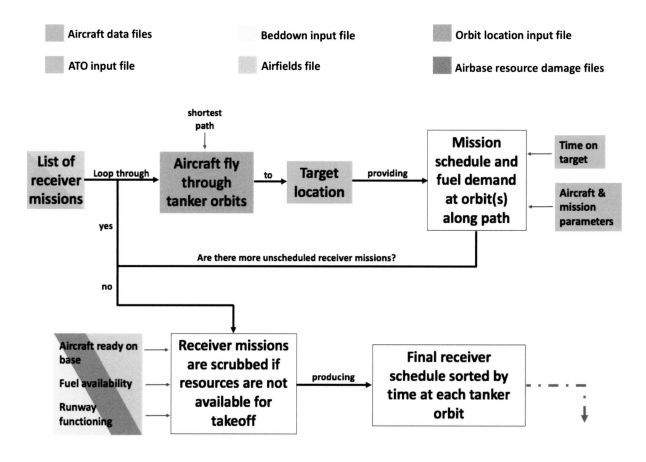

Figure 1.2. Tanker Scheduling

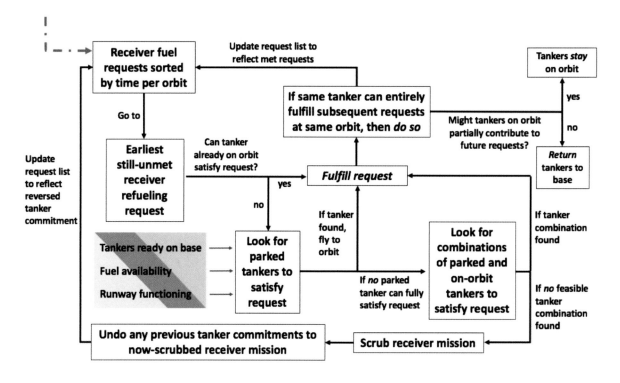

Figure 1.1 shows how KARMA determines whether all receiver missions in the ATO can be launched based on air base resources and the number of aircraft present at each air base. Every receiver sortie has a target destination and time on target specified in the ATO. From a set of possible tanker rendezvous locations provided by the user, KARMA finds a path made up of the smallest number of feasible journey legs and refueling stops that allows the sortie to reach its target; from the fixed time on target, the entire flight schedule of the sortie follows. The feasibility of receiver takeoff times is then checked to make sure that there is enough fuel on base, that there is a long-enough runway available for takeoff, and that there are enough suitable aircraft of the correct mission design system (MDS) available (not in flight and not being maintained). Any receiver sorties that cannot take off are scrubbed. This yields a final receiver schedule, and receiver fuel requests at each orbit are sorted by time.

A tanker schedule is then calculated based on the receiver fuel requests at each orbit. This is depicted in Figure 1.2. A tanker is allocated to refuel the earliest still-unmet receiver refueling request in the following way. First, KARMA evaluates whether any tanker already at the same orbit as the receiver can satisfy at least part of the request. If there are no on-orbit tankers that can fulfill (or partially fulfill) the request, KARMA searches for a tanker at an air base that is available and can provide enough fuel to fulfill either the entire request or the remainder of the request. If one is available, it is scheduled to depart its air base at a certain time so that it can reach the orbit and fulfill the request on time. If no single tanker on the ground can fulfill the request, then combinations of tankers on orbit, or on the ground and on orbit, that can fulfill the request are searched for, and, if such a combination exists, it is used to fulfill the request. The first time a tanker is flown to an orbit to fulfill a request, KARMA checks whether the same tanker can entirely fulfill future requests at the same orbit, and then it fulfills those requests. If there are no other future requests to which the tanker could contribute, it returns to base; if the tanker might partially contribute to future requests, it stays on orbit with its time of return to base not yet determined.

If there is no tanker or combination of tankers that can fulfill a receiver request, then the receiver mission is scrubbed. This forces previous tanker commitments that were made to the now-scrubbed receiver mission to be undone. Because the flight schedules of those tankers are partly undone, any other tankers and receivers that were scheduled to interact with those tankers may also have their schedules partly undone, possibly placing some entries back into the list of unrefueled receiver requests. In this way, tankers are allocated until all receiver requests have either been met or scrubbed and a feasible tanker schedule has been produced.

There are no random draws or stochastic behavior in KARMA itself; the output is determined by the input. If the analyst wishes to consider a range of different possible scenarios (e.g., enemy attacks that are more successful or less successful), it will be necessary to run KARMA once for each possibility with different inputs. Fortunately, KARMA's relatively fast run time should make it feasible to explore the space of possibilities.

This description is only a summary of the KARMA algorithms. The remainder of this report goes into much greater detail about how KARMA works.

Organization of This Report

This chapter has provided a high-level description of KARMA. Readers who simply want to run the model may proceed to Appendix A, which describes the input files and data requirements of the model, and Appendix B, which describes the output files.

For those readers interested in the algorithmic details, Chapter 2 explains how the fuel demand and non-tanker aircraft schedules are calculated. Chapter 3 details the tanker allocation algorithms we used to best satisfy the fuel demand. Chapter 4 discusses how we incorporated the effects of air base attacks in the model. Chapter 5 expounds upon potential future work and concludes the report.

2. Receiver Aircraft Demand

Henceforth, we will call aircraft that are aerially refueled *receivers*. KARMA receives as input a list of receiver missions specifying the air base from which each mission takes off, the intended destination, and the required time of arrival at the destination. From this data, KARMA produces a flight plan for each receiver mission in the ATO that falls within the start and end days of the conflict, as specified in the parameters file. For each mission, KARMA determines the tanker orbits at which the receiver should be refueled, the times at which the receiver must arrive at and depart from those orbits, and the times at which the mission must take off and must return to base.[11] KARMA also calculates the schedules of non-tanker aircraft that do not need to be or cannot be aerially refueled—e.g., the MQ-9—to account for their use of air base fuel resources; those aircraft follow a simple path of home base to target and then back to home base.

KARMA then checks that there will be enough aircraft of the appropriate type ready to conduct each mission, that the air base will have enough fuel, and that there will be a usable runway at the appropriate time for the aircraft to take off. If there is a problem, the receiver mission is scrubbed; otherwise, aircraft tails of the appropriate type are assigned to carry out the mission. The geographic location and availability of each non-tanker tail are tracked for the duration of the war.[12] After flying a sortie and returning to its base, a tail requires a certain amount of time on the ground before it can be used to fly another sortie. This turn time incorporates aircraft maintenance, on-base movement, and on-base refueling. Currently, this turn time is a single value input by the user. Deviations from this turn time could make it impossible for aircraft at an air base to maintain the sortie rates required by the ATO. Excursions that explore ranges of turn time per aircraft are necessary to understand the robustness of the ATO with respect to aircraft turn times.

KARMA then has a schedule of receivers that are expected to arrive at various tanker orbits at known times with known fuel demands. This fuel demand schedule is then passed to KARMA's tanker allocation algorithm, which is described in the next chapter. In the remainder of this chapter, we outline each step in the code that produces the receiver schedule.

---

[11] Takeoff and landing separation at a base are not modeled as a constraint.

[12] As an exception, a squadron of aircraft tails may be reassigned from one base to another over the course of the war. The transportation of the squadron from the first base to the second base is not explicitly modeled; it is just assumed to take place. Also, if an aircraft is forced to divert from its mission, the tail is assumed to return to its squadron, but the means by which this happens is not modeled. Lastly, the precise location of an aircraft in flight between air base and orbit or between orbits is not tracked, although its in-flight status is tracked.

Routing Receiver Aircraft

The first step in producing the schedule of non-tanker aircraft is to route receiver sorties from their home bases to their target locations, and back, through tanker orbits. The locations of *candidate* tanker orbit locations are an input to KARMA. (It is possible that KARMA will not need to route receivers or tankers to every candidate orbit location.) Each receiver has a maximum distance that it can fly, depending on its munitions package, fuel load, and fuel reserve.

KARMA divides the ATO into strike-type and patrol-type missions. For those missions that require tanker support, the great-circle distance that the receiver can travel from its home base to its first tanker orbit is used to determine a set of possible locations for the first tanker rendezvous. Non-tanker aircraft take off with a specified amount of fuel, which may or may not equal the aircraft's full fuel capacity. Also, the user may specify that particular bases with low fuel resources supply non-tanker aircraft with only a fixed fraction of their normal takeoff fuel loads. For both of these reasons, the distance an aircraft can fly to its first tanker orbit may be less than the normal maximum range of the aircraft.

KARMA assumes that aircraft are filled to their full fuel capacity at each tanker orbit. If the ATO specifies that the aircraft is carrying external fuel tanks, these are also filled. However, for flights that consist of more than one aircraft, the first aircraft to be refueled by the tanker will burn some fuel waiting for the other aircraft in the flight to be refueled; therefore, the distance that the multi-aircraft flight can travel between tanker orbits is still somewhat less than the theoretical maximum range of one aircraft. KARMA currently accounts for this with a safety factor so that a one-plane flight does not plan to fly farther than 100 percent of its nominal range, a two-plane flight does not plan to fly farther than 90 percent of the aircraft's nominal range, and a four-plane flight does not plan to fly farther than 80 percent of the aircraft's nominal range.[13]

The final tanker orbit that the receiver visits before arriving at its destination must lie within a radius of the destination equal to half of the distance that a receiver can travel between orbits. Furthermore, the user may specify a minimum or maximum separation between the final tanker orbit and destination. Given all these constraints, KARMA finds a path[14] from the takeoff point to the destination that minimizes the number of tanker stops.[15] Figure 2.1 illustrates all the possible paths that a notional receiver could take to get from its air base to its destination. Each path is drawn in a different color; the paths are shown slightly out of sync with one another to

---

[13] This is a relatively crude estimate, and, in the future, it can be made precise.

[14] KARMA uses the NetworkX Python package, developed primarily at the Los Alamos National Laboratory, to find shortest paths.

[15] Typically, this will product the most direct (shortest path) route as well. We minimized the number of tanker stops because it should generally put the least stress on the tanker force and find the most efficient tanker schedule, given our greedy algorithm.

highlight each unique path. The red path is chosen because it has the fewest tanker stops. Note that KARMA does not currently have the ability to avoid restricted flight areas. Note also that this figure is not drawn to scale.

Figure 2.1. Routing an Aircraft Between Its Air Base and Destination

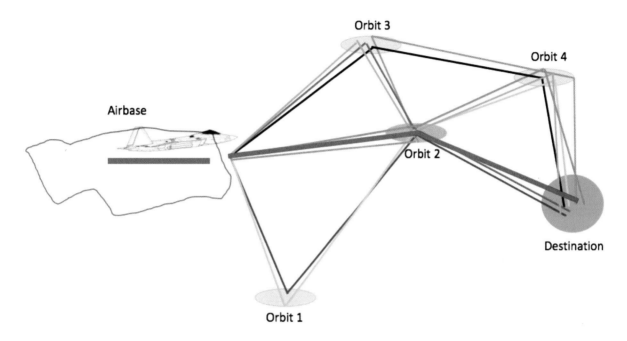

If the set of candidate orbit locations does not contain a first or last orbit that is sufficiently close to the air base or target, or if there is no path for an aircraft given its travel capabilities (performance parameters and current fuel load), then the sortie is marked as impossible and scrubbed.

Determining Fuel Requests at Tanker Orbits from the Receiver Paths

The aircraft are flown through their respective paths for each sortie in the ATO that is modeled. To illustrate how this works, consider the following notional two-ship F-22 sortie flying a mission from Miami to Bermuda through two tanker orbits:

Miami ⇨ Clinton ⇨ Mimas ⇨ Bermuda

The aircraft leave Miami, refuel at Clinton, refuel at Mimas, do patrol in Bermuda (returning to Mimas as necessary to refuel and then returning to Bermuda to continue patrol), and, after the combat air patrol (CAP) portion of the mission is over,[16] the F-22s will top off at Mimas, fly to Clinton to be refueled, and then land back at their home base, Miami. For each stop in this flight history, KARMA records important information, including arrival and departure time at each waypoint and the amount of fuel needed and transferred during aerial refueling stops. In between waypoints, the precise locations and fuel loads of aircraft are not recorded. At this point, KARMA does not attempt to determine which tanker aircraft will rendezvous with the F-22s, but the initial assumption is that tankers will be available.

The two F-22s spend time and fuel going between Miami and Clinton. As described in Chapter 1, the calculation of time and fuel consumed can be fairly detailed, depending on how much performance data are present in the F-22 aircraft data file. The aircraft fly in long-range cruise mode between orbits, if information on that mode is available. (If long-range cruise mode were absent from the data file, KARMA would try to substitute maximum-range cruise, and then maximum endurance.) If no detailed performance data are present in an aircraft data file, then a single fuel-burn value (lb./hr.) is used.[17]

The first F-22 then hooks up with a notional tanker at Clinton, which is assumed to take 2 minutes, and stays on the boom, both burning and receiving fuel, until it gets refueled to its capacity. Meanwhile, the second F-22 waits for its partner to be refueled. Once its partner has been fully refueled, the second F-22 hooks up and receives fuel while the first F-22 waits. Then both aircraft fly on to Mimas, where the refueling process is repeated. Note that, whenever the F-22s depart from a tanker, they have unequal amounts of fuel, because the first fighter to refuel had to wait for the other. The aircraft with the least amount of fuel remaining is the first to refuel when the pair arrives at another tanker.

Once the F-22s reach Bermuda, their behavior depends on whether they are flying a strike or patrol mission. If they are flying a strike mission, they expend their munitions, reducing their weight, and then return to Clinton, where they are topped off by aerial refueling; fly to Mimas, where they are aerially refueled; and finally land back at Miami with whatever fuel they did not expend during the last leg of their missions.

If the F-22s are flying a patrol mission, the KARMA parameters file specifies a desired total time for them to remain on station. Aircraft on station are assumed to fly in maximum endurance mode, if possible. If their fuel capacity allows them to patrol for the desired amount of time without leaving station to refuel, they will do so. However, it may be that the desired total time does not neatly equal a natural number of patrols. For example, suppose that F-22s are desired to spend 120 minutes per sortie on station, but the geometry of the tanker orbit and the fighter's required fuel reserves are such that the F-22s can spend 90 minutes on station at one time before

---

[16] The amount of time the sortie needs to remain on station in Bermuda is set in the parameters file, as described in Appendix A.

[17] In the future, other flight modes corresponding to different performance data could be added. Note that if no fuel-burn information at all is provided, then KARMA cannot run.

returning to a tanker to refuel. If each F-22 had to satisfy the 120-minute requirement, then each F-22 would have to make two visits to its station, but one or both of those visits would be inefficiently short. Instead, to make efficient use of resources, KARMA interprets the 120 minutes on station as only an *average* goal. At any point while constructing the schedule, if all F-22 patrol missions scheduled so far have, on average, fallen short of the goal, then the next F-22 will *exceed* the goal by staying on station for two 90-minute sessions. If all F-22 patrol missions scheduled so far have, on average, exceeded the goal, the next F-22 mission will be scheduled to fall short of the goal by staying on station for only one 90-minute session. In this way, some F-22 sorties spend more time on station, and some spend less, but the average should converge to be close to the specified goal.

The time that the F-22s must first arrive at Bermuda is fixed by the ATO. If this particular F-22 sortie required two CAP sessions at Bermuda, it visited Mimas a total of three times: once on the outbound trip, once on the homebound trip, and once during its CAP. It would have visited Clinton twice: once on the outbound trip and once on the homebound trip. For each stop at a tanker orbit, KARMA has calculated the fuel transferred to the two F-22s and the amount of time that the F-22s spent on the tanker boom on each occasion. From this, KARMA determines the times that the F-22s arrive and depart from the tanker orbits and the times that they leave and return to Miami.

Once aircraft land, they require a turnaround time, specified in the aircraft data file, for ground refueling and maintenance.[18]

Checking the Feasibility of the Receiver Schedule

Once the schedule and fuel requirements of all of the receivers (and non–aerially refueled aircraft) have been calculated, the feasibility of the schedule is checked to make sure that there are aircraft available to fly the missions, as well as the necessary air base resources. This check is first performed for all planned receiver takeoffs at the beginning of the scenario to assess the feasibility of the initial war plan. As the simulation progresses, Red attacks may occur and damage some Blue air bases, at which time KARMA will perform the check again to see which remaining Blue receiver takeoffs can be supported by remaining air base resources.

The fuel available at air bases can be specified either by the airfields file (which assigns an initial fuel amount on base plus a resupply each day) or by the fuel damage and resupply file (which assigns an initial fuel amount plus resupply amounts at given times)—or both. KARMA

---

[18] Note that KARMA does not currently include turnaround congestion. Furthermore, in the case of air base attacks (detailed in Chapter 4), turnaround times do not increase. In reality, air base attacks would probably cause additional delays in aircraft turn rates. In these ways, KARMA is likely overestimating the potential for aircraft to be ready to launch.

then loops through all missions in order of takeoff time and determines whether the aircraft takeoff can happen. Figure 2.2 illustrates the procedure.

First, KARMA checks that the home air base of the mission has a long-enough runway open to support the aircraft. If all the base runways are too short or are closed because of enemy action at the time of takeoff, then the mission is scrubbed.[19] Then KARMA determines whether the air base has sufficient fuel in storage to provide the aircraft with its specified takeoff fuel load;[20] if it does not, the mission is scrubbed.

Finally, KARMA checks for aircraft availability on the base. If a mission requires two F-22s, then there must be two F-22 tails that are available—stationed at the base, not in maintenance, not destroyed, and not in flight. If there are multiple available tails that could be used, KARMA preferentially chooses tails that have already flown more missions. If, at the end of the conflict, some aircraft tails were never used, this would imply a degree of slack in the schedule.

If there are not enough aircraft available to fly the mission, then the mission is scrubbed. The number of minutes until enough aircraft *would* have been ready to fly is noted in KARMA output. This should give the user a sense of whether the mission *would* have been feasible with a slightly faster aircraft turnaround time or slight schedule adjustments in the ATO or whether there is a more fundamental lack of aircraft necessary to carry out the ATO.[21]

Those receiver missions that can be supported by base resources are scheduled for takeoff, and air base fuel is set aside to fuel those aircraft. Because KARMA does this resource allocation prior to constructing the tanker schedule, KARMA gives receiver aircraft first claim on air base fuel resources. Tanker missions must be planned using the air base fuel that has not already been allocated to receivers.

---

[19] The modeling of runway closure due to air base attack is described fully in Chapter 4.

[20] Aircraft have normal takeoff fuel loads specified in the aircraft input file. In addition, an air base may be designated (in the airfields input file) to provide aircraft with only a fraction of their normal fuel loads, as previously discussed.

[21] Of course, if we did attempt to add "slack" to the system and have receiver sorties take off a few minutes late because an aircraft was about to be ready, then that aircraft might not be able to fly the next mission to which it was ultimately assigned. The entire assessment of which aircraft flew which receiver mission and which missions were scrubbed would likely shift a bit.

Figure 2.2. Checking the Availability of Air Base Resources for Receiver Sorties

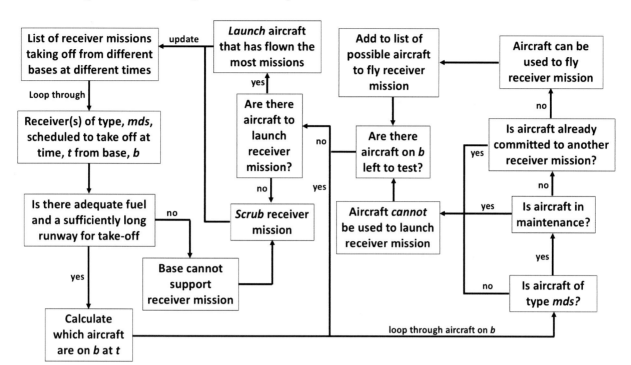

Scheduling Refueling Requests

KARMA now has a list of receiver missions that can feasibly fly *if* there are sufficient tanker aircraft to meet the necessary refueling rendezvous. There is also a set of scrubbed missions if there were insufficient resources to support the receiver missions. The missions that do fly correspond to a series of fuel requests at different tanker orbits at various times throughout the conflict days that are simulated. These requests are grouped by tanker orbit and then sorted from earliest to latest. These tanker orbit schedules are the starting point for the tanker allocation algorithms described in the next chapter.

3. Tanker Allocation

At this point, a nominal receiver schedule has been established, and the times and locations at which certain receiver aircraft are expecting tanker support are known. The numbers and types of tanker aircraft based in certain locations are also assumed to be known. The problem now is to allocate the available tanker aircraft to efficiently meet the requests for aerial refueling.

Because the tanker base locations and the orbit locations where tankers will rendezvous with receivers have already been determined, it is convenient to start by calculating the following for each type of tanker at each tanker base and for each possible orbit:

- the amount of fuel that type of tanker is able to carry off of the base, assuming that the runways are open and usable for their full nominal length
- the flight time and fuel required for the tanker to reach the orbit
- the amount of fuel that that type of tanker will need to return to base with acceptable reserves—and thus, implicitly, the maximum offloadable fuel that can be delivered by each tanker type–base–orbit combination.

Each tanker type–base–orbit combination is scored by the maximum amount of offloadable fuel that can be delivered divided by the minimum tanker-hours required for the tanker to fly to the orbit, return to base, and be refueled and maintained for another mission. In general, KARMA will try to use the tanker–orbit combinations with the highest scores in order to deliver the maximum usable fuel per tanker-hour.

Whether a request comes from one receiver aircraft or a flight of multiple receiver aircraft, only one tanker aircraft responds to a refueling request at a time and refuels the receivers in series. If the first tanker aircraft does not have sufficient fuel to meet the entire request, it should be supplemented by a second tanker aircraft that continues the refueling.

If it is desired for multiple tankers to refuel receivers in parallel—for example, if a flight of four fighters should be met by two tankers that refuel the fighters in parallel—then the request should be divided into multiple requests; e.g., the flight of four fighters should be divided into two flights of two fighters each for KARMA's purposes.

Tanker Allocation Algorithm

KARMA plans an allocation of the available tankers as follows. Every aerial refueling request in the ATO is sorted into chronological order. As KARMA considers the earliest refueling request that has not yet been handled:

1. If there is already a tanker aircraft on orbit or expected to be on orbit prior to the arrival of the receiver, with sufficient unallocated fuel, a compatible boom or drogue, and

available time to meet the refueling request, then that tanker will be assigned to the request.

2. Otherwise, KARMA searches for a tanker on the ground.[22] Each of the possible tanker types and tanker bases is considered in decreasing order of score based on maximum offloadable fuel divided by minimum tanker-hours required. If an option is found such that a tanker with the appropriate boom or drogue is available for takeoff at the appropriate time and can deliver enough fuel to meet the request, and there are no other obstacles (there is a usable runway and the base has sufficient fuel), then that tanker is scheduled to fly to the orbit and meet the request. That tanker tail is then marked as busy and cannot be assigned to any other orbits until after it has returned to base from the orbit under consideration.

3. If no single tanker on the ground or in the air can deliver enough fuel to fully satisfy the request, whichever available tanker—either on the ground or already present at the orbit—can deliver the *most* fuel to the receiver is assigned to do so. The algorithm then returns to step 1 to find another tanker to supply the remaining fuel need. In this way, two or more tankers can be scheduled to meet a single large refueling request in sequence.[23]

4. If *no* available tanker can be found to complete the refueling of the receiver, it is not possible to satisfy the refueling request with the remaining available tankers, and the receiver mission is scrubbed.

    a. If the receiver is already in flight (i.e., the receiver took off on the supposition that it would have tanker support, but something has changed, perhaps due to Red attacks, and now tanker support is not available), then the receiver is assumed to be diverted after any aerial refuelings that have already taken place. The exact process by which the diverted receiver is recovered and makes its way back to its home base is not currently modeled in KARMA.

    b. It may be that some tankers were already scheduled to support the receiver mission at certain points, but those refuelings had not yet happened. Now that the receiver mission is scrubbed, the schedules for those tankers should also be revised. Assuming that KARMA is searching for an efficient solution, those tanker schedules are undone back to the point before the scheduled rendezvous with the canceled receiver. (Of course, no events can be undone that are considered to have already happened.) Any still-valid refueling requests that were

---

[22] The process by which a tanker is deemed available is the same described for receivers in Chapter 2 and as depicted in Figure 2.1, with a few crucial differences. First, a tanker can take off partially full from a base that does not meet runway length requirements. Second, the tanker must have adequate fuel to refuel the request (either alone or in concert with other tankers). Third, it must have the necessary boom or drogue.

[23] Note that, although this strategy may not maximize the number of receiver missions that can be completed, it is essential for large aircraft.

scheduled to be met by those tankers after the canceled requests have now been undone, and the process of allocating tanker(s) to those still-valid requests must be redone; those requests are effectively reinserted back into the list of requests to handle.

5. If a tanker was available and scheduled to meet the refueling request, KARMA then looks ahead to see whether there are other subsequent refueling requests at the same orbit that the tanker could also fully meet. If so, the tanker will be scheduled to meet those requests also. This look-ahead feature is important because it efficiently ensures that tankers are returned back to base if they are not needed any longer at an orbit. This will make them available for another mission sooner than if they stayed on orbit unnecessarily.

6. Within their bingo limits, tankers remain allocated to an orbit as long as there are unhandled refueling requests at that orbit to which they might still contribute some fuel. (The bingo time at each mission stage is the latest time that it can be on orbit before it must depart the orbit.[24]) Once all such requests have been handled, a tanker is scheduled to return to base. If it has some surplus fuel above its required reserves, and if there is another tanker at the orbit that can be aerially refueled, it may transfer its surplus fuel to that other tanker, as described later in this chapter.

This process is repeated until every receiver mission either has been allocated sufficient tanker support or has been scrubbed because of a lack of feasible tanker support. Once tanker allocation is completed, there is a wealth of information known about every tanker and receiver: what orbits they visit at what times and how much fuel is transferred between tanker and receiver aircraft tails. As an example of what an orbit might experience, consider Figure 3.1, which is an example of a rainbow chart used by AMC planners. This particular figure visualizes four hours of time at a notional tanker orbit. The blue bars on the top of the figure represent three different tankers that arrive and leave during this period. The red bars on the bottom half of the figure represent four receiver missions that arrive and leave during this period.[25] Each bar is annotated by a line of text indicating

- minute of arrival after the hour
- number of aircraft
- aircraft type
- fuel load on arrival (for tankers) or total fuel onload required (for receiver flights)
- minute of departure after the hour

---

[24] It does not have a bingo time at takeoff because it has not yet left its home base.

[25] The receiver arrival times are determined by their respective aircraft flight profiles and by their required times on target as specified in the receiver ATO. There is no additional attempt to coordinate the arrival times of different receivers at a refueling orbit. Thus, as in this case, three tankers may be required to serve three receiver missions that arrive at almost the same time.

Thus the text "9/1 KC-46A/204K/22" indicates that one KC-46A is scheduled to arrive at 23:09 with 204,000 lb. of fuel and depart at 23:22. It is therefore available to serve "9/1 E-3A/67K/22," one E-3A aircraft that arrives at 23:09, receives 67,000 lb. of fuel, and departs at 23:22. Two EA-18G aircraft arrive at 23:11 requiring a total of 17,000 lb. of fuel between them, so a second tanker must fly to the orbit to refuel them. Three minutes later, one E-8C arrives requesting 53,000 lb. of fuel, requiring a third tanker to be available to service it. After these aircraft leave, there is more than a two-and-a-half-hour gap before the next receiver mission arrives (two EA-18Gs at 02:02); the first tanker does not have enough fuel to meet that request, but the tanker that arrived at 23:11 has only offloaded 17,000 lb. and can wait to rendezvous with the next set of EA-18Gs at 02:02. The other two tankers are sent back to their home bases so that they can be reused efficiently, as tankers should not stay on the orbit if there are not going to be any receivers arriving for them to aerially refuel.[26] The length of each receiver bar indicates how long aerial refueling took at that orbit.

Figure 3.1. Notional Rainbow Chart

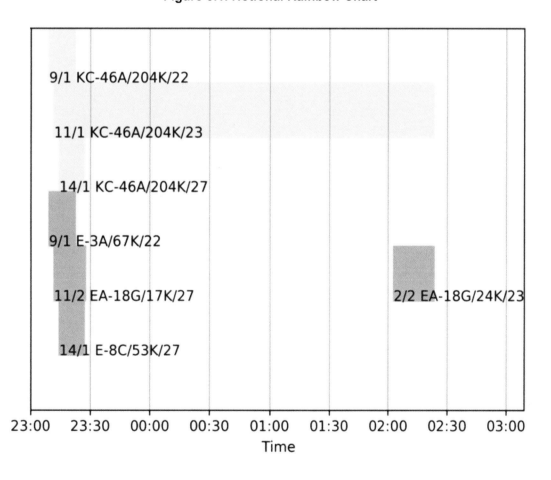

---

[26] This, of course, assumes that there is no desire to keep tankers in the air for some other reason, such as to avoid being struck by missiles during an attack or to keep them safe from ground attack.

Reduced Computation but Less-Efficient Solution

KARMA allocates tankers to meet receiver requests in a relatively "greedy" fashion, but when it encounters a receiver sortie that it cannot completely support with the available tankers, it backtracks and reassigns any tankers that were previously allocated to that receiver sortie. This makes better use of available tanker resources, at the expense of increased computation by KARMA.

In certain circumstances, the user may want a "quick and dirty" answer from KARMA. Therefore, KARMA has an optional parameter setting in which KARMA does not backtrack to reconsider tanker allocations once made. If it turns out that the tanker fleet cannot completely support a receiver mission, then the receiver mission is scrubbed as in step 4 above, but tankers that were already scheduled to support the receiver mission are not rescheduled as in step 4.b. This makes KARMA arrive at a solution much faster, but, of course, the resulting solution will have made a less efficient use of tanker or fuel resources. The trade-off between run time and solution quality is at the user's discretion.

Tanker Range Extension by En Route Buddy Tanking

If the user enables en route buddy tanking, KARMA will also consider pairing tankers so that one refuels the other en route to its orbit. This can be a more effective way to deliver fuel to orbits distant from the tanker base(s). KARMA considers every possible pairing of tanker types and bases, given the tanker laydown in the scenario. The recipient tanker must be of a type that can be aerially refueled; the donor tanker can be of any type.

For each possible recipient tanker–base–donor tanker–base–orbit combination, KARMA calculates the meet point at which the donor tanker from base A should rendezvous with and transfer fuel to the recipient tanker from base B. KARMA uses the Broyden-Fletcher-Goldfarb-Shanno numerical solver (SciPy, 2017) to find a meet point that maximizes the fuel delivered by the recipient tanker to the final orbit and, secondarily, minimizes the total flight time of the two tankers.

It is possible that both tankers take off from the same base. In that case, both tankers travel in the direction of the final orbit, and the meet point at which the fuel transfer takes place will be the point en route at which the recipient tanker has consumed enough fuel that it can accept all of the donor tanker's remaining surplus fuel, leaving the donor tanker just enough to return to base.

For a given combination of orbit and tanker locations, it may be that there is no optimal meet point en route. In particular, it may be that the two tankers can deliver more fuel to the end orbit by both flying there and there is no benefit to transferring fuel en route. Such cases are discarded as possible en route buddy tanking combinations. (It still might be useful for the two tankers to transfer fuel while they are on orbit, but this strategy is handled separately.)

KARMA then considers all viable buddy tanking combinations together with single-tanker options when deciding which available tankers to send to an orbit. Because en route buddy tanking makes sense only if at least one tanker is based far from the destination orbit and the pair of tankers will use many total flight-hours, en route buddy tanking will usually not be chosen if there are any single-tanker options available. But if no available single tanker can satisfy a distant refueling request, KARMA will select an available en route buddy tanking option that does so.

Intra-Orbital Fuel Transfers Between Tankers

If KARMA has scheduled two or more tankers to be present at an orbit at the same time, it must be because the additional tankers were necessary to meet requests that the first tanker could not meet alone. However, once those requests are past, it may no longer be desirable to keep multiple tankers on orbit, unnecessarily consuming fuel and tanker flight-hours. As described above, KARMA schedules an orbiting tanker to return to base if there are no upcoming refueling requests for which it is needed—perhaps because other tankers on orbit have been scheduled to supply all upcoming requests.

When KARMA is scheduling an orbiting tanker to return to base, the tanker may still have residual surplus fuel beyond its necessary reserves, and it may be wasteful for the tanker to return to base with this surplus fuel. The most efficient strategy may be to consolidate the tanker's surplus fuel in those tankers that remain on orbit to meet later receiver demands. If the user has enabled intra-orbital fuel transfers, then KARMA checks whether there are any other tankers that can be aerially refueled and that are scheduled to occupy the same orbit as the returning tanker at any overlapping times. If so, KARMA attempts to finds times when the tankers are colocated and not occupied with receivers so a transfer of the surplus fuel from one tanker to the other can be scheduled. The fuel histories of both donor and recipient tankers are modified. The on-orbit time of the recipient tanker(s) may now be extended. If two tankers at the same orbit are both candidates to return to base and only one of them can be aerially refueled, KARMA prefers to send the non–aerially refuelable tanker home first (because of the possibility that the aerially refuelable tanker's mission might still be extended by a fuel donation). If there is a choice of possible recipient tankers, KARMA prefers to transfer fuel to the one with the least on-board fuel.

Chapters 2 and 3 described how the receiver schedule and tanker ATO are calculated given resource limitations inherent to the scenario setup. Air base attacks can starkly change the amount of resources available to aircraft. How the damage from air base attacks (and the effect on sortie generation) is incorporated into KARMA is described in the next chapter.

4. Air Base Attacks

The algorithms described thus far calculate the schedules of the receiver force and the tanker ATO for a scenario without including air base attacks. Air base attacks can change the dynamics of the scenario significantly when important resources are destroyed. KARMA models the effects of attacks on fuel, runways, and parked aircraft because these directly affect tankers.[27] As described in Appendix A, damage to fuel and aircraft and runway closures are inputted into KARMA via damage input files, which can be calculated by TAB-VAM.[28] An accompanying script transforms TAB-VAM damage outputs to KARMA input files. Damage events occur at specified times. It is important to note that KARMA does not use any foreknowledge of attacks when planning the tanker ATO. This is imperative for accurately modeling two possible situations.

First, after a receiver mission takes off as scheduled, an enemy attack could create a situation in which no tanker can take off to rendezvous with the receiver aircraft as previously expected. The receiver aircraft thus cannot finish their mission and have to be diverted. KARMA has to accurately account for the resources used by the receiver and by any tankers supporting the receiver prior to diversion. It would be unrealistic to avoid the situation by planning around the upcoming attack.

Second, tanker missions may take off to support a scheduled receiver mission, which is then scrubbed because of an enemy attack, so that the tanker aircraft arrives at a rendezvous with no receiver. KARMA can make different use of the tanker after it arrives at its orbit, but it cannot undo the fact that the tanker took off prior to the attack in the first place.

Thus, KARMA starts by calculating the receiver schedule and tanker ATO assuming *no* missile attacks. The receiver schedule does not change prior to the time of an attack. From this point forward, the receiver schedule is rechecked to ascertain whether aircraft can take off—this time taking into account resource degradation from the air base attack. Tanker rendezvous prior to the attack event are not affected. Tankers that have taken off and are in flight proceed to their

---

[27] KARMA does not currently model maintenance delays as a result of attacks, although the user can adjust the ground turnaround time for aircraft in the aircraft data files as a proxy for maintenance delays. A weakness of this approach is that it would affect the turnaround time for the duration of the simulation. There is not currently a way to change this value mid-conflict, although this is a feature that would be relatively easy to add.

[28] Of course, TAB-VAM does not have to be used to generate air base damage. Analysts might actually prefer creating a set of damage input files to sweep over a range of resource degradation. Other models that estimate air base damage from attack can also be used, and the results can be translated into the file format that KARMA requires. An example of an alternative to TAB-VAM is the Air Force Research Laboratory's Air Base Attack Tool (ABAT).

planned orbits, even if they are no longer needed because of receiver mission cancellations.[29] Then, the tanker schedule is recalculated from the time of the attack in response to the change in the receiver schedule and allowing for the effects of any destroyed tankers, destroyed air base fuel, or closed runways.

For computational efficiency, KARMA does use preknowledge of the attack schedule to the following extent: KARMA replans the tanker ATO to a point 24 hours past only the *next* attack. The 24-hour window provides sufficient cushion that tanker and receiver missions are planned without undue clairvoyance, to avoid the pitfalls described above, but KARMA does not produce an entire new campaign plan that will be overcome by events. This process is repeated, recalculating both the receiver schedule and tanker ATO every time there are new air base attacks.

Calculating the tanker ATO requires that all damage events are translated into degraded resources. As described in Chapter 2, the fuel damage file contains the time of the attack, the base being attacked, and the amount of fuel that is destroyed. KARMA maintains a fuel history for each air base. This fuel history contains fuel supplies to the base, fuel draws at the base when aircraft take off, and fuel damage events at the base due to air base attacks. The fuel history makes it possible to know exactly how much fuel is available at the base at any time in the simulation. KARMA refers to this history when determining whether aircraft will have sufficient fuel to take off. Figure 4.1 shows a notional fuel history of an air base over time. This particular base received fuel at the start of the simulation and, over time, had multiple fuel draws by aircraft taking off, and it eventually runs out of fuel. The base could have been resupplied with fuel, but we did not include this option for this example.

---

[29] This is a point of inefficiency in the model; it is possible that a tanker would not have to arrive at its orbit just to be sent home but could be revectored in real time.

Figure 4.1. Notional Fuel History at an Air Base over Time

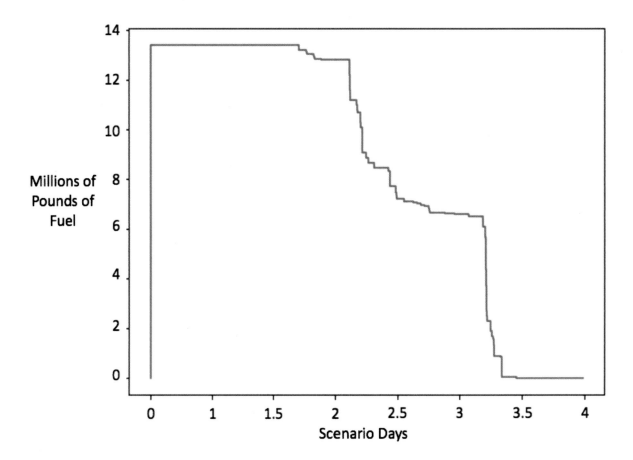

The runway availability input file delineates the damage to runways due to attack at air bases over time. Runways are closed for a specified number of hours at the base being attacked, starting from the time of attack. Runways can be closed to large aircraft, to small aircraft, or to both, and the number of hours of closure can be different for large and small aircraft.

Damage to sheltered and unsheltered parked aircraft is calculated separately. Unsheltered aircraft are damaged according to the missile ramp coverage. When a warhead is aimed at parked aircraft, some area of the parking ramp is affected. This affected area is inputted as a fraction of the total parking ramp area. For example, if a base has 1,000 square feet of parking area, and 300 square feet were hit by missile fragments, then there is 30-percent ramp coverage. KARMA tracks exactly which aircraft are in flight and which are on the ground at the time of attack. KARMA calculates the expected number of aircraft destroyed as the ramp coverage fraction multiplied by the number of aircraft on the ground that are not sheltered. Each MDS is considered separately for this purpose, and no MDS is more vulnerable than any other.

The expected total number of destroyed tails of each MDS is tracked throughout the campaign, and fractional expected kills are rounded off in the following way. If a series of missile attacks resulted in the expected destruction of 0.3 aircraft of a given MDS, then no aircraft of that MDS are treated as destroyed, and all tails can continue to carry out missions. If

24

another missile attack brings the total expected aircraft kills to a number between 0.5 and 1.5, then one of the tails of that MDS parked at the attacked base is marked destroyed and can no longer be used. If the running total of expected kills is between 1.5 and 2.5, a second aircraft of that MDS is marked destroyed, and so on. In other words, the cumulative expected total of aircraft damage is rounded to the nearest integer.

Sheltered aircraft are not affected by parking ramp coverage, but they can be damaged if they are inside shelters that get destroyed. Aircraft are automatically put in shelters in a prioritized order, accounting for the size of the aircraft and shelter availability. For small aircraft, F-22 aircraft have the highest priority, followed by F-35s, followed by fourth-generation fighters. For large aircraft, B-2s and long-range strike platforms have the highest priority, followed by E-3s, E-8s, and tankers, then followed by other large aircraft. If a shelter is destroyed, it is assumed that the aircraft inside is also damaged. If few aircraft are on base at the time of attack, it is possible that a base could have empty shelters that get hit during an attack. In this case, there would be no damage to aircraft, although the shelters would be permanently damaged, and aircraft could no longer be sheltered in them.

5. Future Work and Conclusions

The work described thus far represents KARMA as it existed in September 2017. KARMA tracks receiver aircraft sorties throughout a campaign on a tail-by-tail basis and assigns tanker sorties to aerially refuel them. Sorties can be completed only if aircraft, fuel, and runway resources are available. This chapter looks to the future and describes new features that could augment KARMA's capabilities and make it even higher fidelity without significantly sacrificing speed and flexibility.

Options for Future Developments

Relaxation of Receiver Scheduling

A general limitation of KARMA currently is that it does not allow any tolerance in receiver mission scheduling. An aircraft must be available to fly a mission at the specified time—not one minute later—or the mission is scrubbed. When a receiver flight arrives at a tanker orbit, a tanker must be available to refuel it immediately—not one minute later—or the mission is scrubbed. The tanker must have enough fuel to completely refuel the receiver flight—not one bit less—or the mission is scrubbed. One can imagine scenarios in which KARMA would make bad decisions over ridiculously small amounts of time or fuel.

In defense of this apparent rigidity, it can be argued that the mission requirements already include some margin for error and that adding some tolerance to the requirements would merely create a new boundary point at which missions must either be supported or abandoned.

Nevertheless, future versions of KARMA could usefully consider more-flexible planning. Currently, KARMA has a "receiver-first" approach, in which the receiver demands are established as a given and then the tanker fleet must try to support them. The only time receiver demands are reduced is when a receiver mission is scrubbed. A future version of KARMA should be able to explore intermediate options—e.g., could the receiver complete its mission with a slightly altered timing of its flight plan? Or could the receiver still succeed in its mission with a partial refuel instead of a complete refuel?

Automatic Placement or Pruning of Candidate Tanker Orbits

Currently, candidate locations for tanker orbits are supplied as inputs to KARMA. If the number of candidate locations is very large, then, in principle, KARMA might spread tankers over too many locations (although, in fact, we have not observed this problem in practice). If the number of candidate locations is small, some locations might see a dangerous density of aircraft, and some receivers might not have good refueling options.

Ideally, a future version of KARMA will automatically adjust tanker orbit locations so that two nearby orbits can be consolidated for efficiency or a different tanker orbit location can be added to relieve congestion or to provide a better option for a receiver mission.

Modeling Diverted Aircraft

If a receiver aircraft is already in flight when circumstances change such that no tanker can make a needed rendezvous, KARMA simply marks the receiver as diverted and ends the mission. In reality, the receiver would have to be diverted to rendezvous with some other tanker or land at a nearby air base and would have to somehow return to its home base. KARMA does not currently model these events.

Furthermore, although KARMA tracks runway closures insofar as they prevent takeoffs, KARMA does not track whether runway closures might prevent aircraft landings. Aircraft returning from a mission are assumed to somehow find a way to land and are available to be used at their home base after the normal period of ground maintenance (e.g., the turnaround time).

In the future, KARMA could include a more sophisticated model of what happens to aircraft tails that are forced to divert from their planned schedules. This could include a chance of an aircraft crashing.

Detailed Air Base Modeling

In reality, aircraft move around on an air base, from the runway, to maintenance shelters if necessary, to parking areas, to munitions loading zones, and then back to a taxiway. This movement is not currently represented in KARMA. A missile attack against parked aircraft thus possibly overestimates damage because not all aircraft currently on the ground are in open parking areas or in shelters.

Pipelines, fuel trucks, and other fuel infrastructure are not modeled in detail in KARMA, although the user could model the effect of attacks on an air base's fuel supply by adjusting the amount of fuel supplied to air bases in the days after an attack.

Future versions of KARMA could include a more detailed model of air base operations and include more-granular representations of important resources.

Adding Other Constraints on Sortie Generation

There are many possible constraints on sortie generation that are not explicitly modeled in KARMA but that could be added.

Munitions Tracking

Currently, munitions are considered in KARMA only as sources of extra weight for receiver aircraft. In reality, munitions supplies are limited by adversary missile attack, by attrition when aircraft drop ordnance, and by the total Air Force munitions inventory and allocation of munitions to a specific fight. KARMA does not track munitions and assumes that combat aircraft always have access to the planned munitions. In reality, if munitions are attrited at an unexpectedly high rate (e.g., because of Red missile attack), combat aircraft missions would be canceled because of unavailability of munitions, which would, in turn, decrease tanker demand.

Detailed Maintenance Modeling

KARMA does not model the maintenance of aircraft in detail, using a fixed ground turnaround time, depending on MDS. In the future, this could be modeled in a much more detailed fashion, depending on maintenance resources on different bases (e.g., large teams versus small teams, the number of maintenance facilities and spare parts available) and the extent of maintenance needed (for example, an aircraft might be damaged but reparable). Furthermore, missile attacks on air base facilities can also affect maintenance and repair capabilities on an air base and could be included in future versions of KARMA.

Runway Usage

Runways are currently tracked as available or unavailable because of missile attack (or for other reasons, such as maintenance); this information is provided in the runway availability input file. Runways must be both open and sufficiently long for an aircraft to take off. KARMA does not currently deconflict takeoff times and could allow multiple flights to take off from the same runway simultaneously.

Command and Control Aircraft

KARMA does not consider the dependency of combat aircraft on command-and-control (C2) aircraft, such as the E-3 or E-8. If these important large aircraft are destroyed or otherwise prevented from flying, this would significantly hinder the capability of fighters and other combat aircraft. A future version of KARMA might scrub combat sorties if there are no E-3 or E-8 aircraft available to provide C2.

Final Thoughts

We have laid out the capabilities and underlying algorithms of KARMA version 1.0, as well as future directions for research and development. KARMA provides tanking solutions for a conflict at a higher level of fidelity than campaign models, such as STORM, or air base attack models, such as TAB-VAM or ABAT. It is not, however, as complex as ARCEM and is not intended for tanker planning in real-world situations. KARMA provides a flexible platform to see the effects of new tanker designs, experiment with tanker CONOPSs and basing schemes, and quickly explore the operational effects of resource degradation due to air base attacks. KARMA offers potential advantages over other models because it is adaptable enough to implement these types of concepts while the subtleties of tanker demand are not lost in a "tanker cloud" or "averaged" approach to aerial refueling. KARMA is also good at illustrating combat tempo because it tracks every single aircraft tail in the simulation and the resulting effect on tanker operations.

KARMA has its limitations as well. Its approach to building a feasible ATO is somewhat greedy. It attempts to allocate tanker resources to meet the earliest unmet need in the ATO schedule. Once resources are allocated to a given receiver, they are not reallocated unless some related mission proves impossible to support and has to be scrubbed from the ATO. Generally speaking, if two missions in the ATO are competing for the same scarce resource, KARMA could be said to favor the earlier mission. KARMA does not have a concept of strategically scrubbing an earlier mission because a later mission in the ATO is more important. Future iterations of KARMA should include new capabilities and could address some of these limitations.

Appendix A. Input Files and Data

KARMA affords users a great deal of flexibility to change scenarios and see how those changes affect tanking requirements and overall airpower generation abilities. We designed KARMA to work well with STORM and TAB-VAM. Data from those models can be used as inputs to KARMA to determine the actions of the Blue combat air force and the effect of Red missile attacks on Blue bases. KARMA then evaluates the ability of the tanker fleet to support the combat air force under those conditions. This appendix describes all of the input files that a user needs to understand and be able to manipulate to use KARMA.

KARMA Parameters File

KARMA reads all inputs from the *data* directory. All input files are in the comma-separated value (CSV) file format. The top input file is parameters.csv, which pulls information from a set of files that the user is intended to change for different scenarios. The parameters file is the only variable input file whose name cannot change. The first part of parameters.csv outlines scenario information, as shown in Table A.1.

Table A.1. Scenario Section of KARMA Parameters File

Scenario Information	Notional Input	Description
Scenario Name	Bermuda Scenario	Name of scenario
Output Classification Level	UNCLASSIFIED	Highest level of classification of all input data
Output Folder Name	Output	Name of output folder
ATO File	Unclassified_ATO	ATO file name; .csv accepted but not required
Airfield Data Sheet	Airfields	File name that contains airfield information; .csv accepted but not required
Beddown File	TotalBeddown	Beddown file name; .csv accepted but not required
Tanker Orbits File	Orbits	Tanker orbits file name; .csv accepted but not required
Start Day	0	Defines the first sortie simulated from the ATO (based on time on target)
End Day	3	Defines the last sortie simulated from the ATO (based on time on target)

The second part of parameters.csv, shown in Table A.2, provides pointers to files that contain damage to airfields and resources due to air base attack. These files can be generated by TAB-VAM. TAB-VAM has been developed at RAND over the past six years to model air bases under kinetic attack. An analyst can run TAB-VAM to determine the extent of damage to aircraft, fuel, and runways in the scenario for different cases. This output can then be automatically converted to KARMA input files by a script.

Table A.2. Air Base Attack Section of KARMA Parameters File

Air Base Attack Files	Notional Input	Description
Case	Baseline-US	Name of case for all input parameters that go into calculating air base damage
Allocation	Cruise-missiles against-fuel	Combination of threat vectors that caused damage
Aircraft Damage File	aircraft_damage	Aircraft damage file name; .csv accepted but not required
Runway Damage File	runway_availability	Runway availability file name; .csv accepted but not required
Fuel Damage/Supply File	fuel_damage_supply	Fuel damage and supply file name; .csv accepted but not required

The third section of parameters.csv contains a set of control flags that can be set to true or false.[30] The effect of these flags is detailed in the "Description" column of Table A.3.

---

[30] *F, FALSE, f, false, False, 0, No, NO, no, n,* and *N* are understood as false; any other entry registers as true.

Table A.3. Control Flag Section of KARMA Parameters File

Control Flags	Notional Input		Description
Use Precalculated Receiver Plan	T	Bermuda_0.pkl	If true, uses .pkl file (here, Bermuda_0.pkl) to load all variables and skips the first part of simulation that routes and schedules receiver aircraft. True should be used if the user wants to calculate tanker plans for different air base attack scenarios. False should be used if anything that affects receiver planning (e.g., orbit locations, beddown) changes.
Save Receiver Plan	F	Bermuda_1.pkl	If true, .pkl file (here, Bermuda_1.pkl) is saved and can be used if "Use Precalculated Receiver Plan" is true. If false, associated .pkl file is ignored.
Allow Buddy Tanking	F		If true, buddy tanking is turned on.
Run Base Attacks	T		If true, damage characterized in air base attack files is used.
Take Fuel Supplies from VAM	T		If true, initial fuel supply and fuel resupply to airfield are taken from fuel_damage_supply.csv.
Take Fuel Supplies from Airfield Data Sheet	F		If true, initial fuel supply and fuel resupply to airfield are taken from airfields.csv.
Count CAP Refuel Trips as Time on Station	F		If true, the time receivers spend traveling between their patrol areas and tankers and time spent aerial refueling are included as time spent on station; if false, *only* the time spent in patrol areas is counted as time on station.
Plot Figures	F		If true, output figures are printed; set to false to speed up simulation.
Prefer Fast Suboptimal Solution	F		If true, tanker solution is calculated less optimally; only set to true if a rough answer is desired very quickly.

The final section of parameters.csv contains important aircraft mission parameters for each MDS (Table A.4). For each MDS, the user can specify different parameters for patrol-type missions and strike-type missions. The default mission parameters are used for any MDS not otherwise specified here.

The first parameter is the required CAP minutes on station, which is the amount of time an aircraft of a certain MDS and mission type should spend on station at its target location. The target location is a representative coordinate of the CAP area (for a patrol mission) or a coordinate from which to release ordnance (for a strike mission). Depending on the setting of the "Count CAP Refuel Trips as Time on Station" control flag (see Table A.3), time spent refueling at the nearest tanker orbit may or may not be counted toward time on station. As described further in Chapter 3, individual aircraft may spend more or less time on station than their required CAP minutes on station, but KARMA will try to make the average time on station converge to this value.

Minimum tanker separation distance defines the closest allowable location of a tanker rendezvous for a tanker refueling a receiver near its final target location. The intent here is that refueling might not be allowed to occur too close to a combat area. The maximum tanker separation distance defines the farthest allowable location of a tanker orbit for a tanker refueling a receiver near its final target location.

The fuel reserve parameter is the lowest number of pounds of fuel that an aircraft can have in its fuel tank. Alternatively, the fuel reserve can be specified as a certain amount of flight time, in the formulation "*x* hours flight time" or "*x* minutes flight time," and KARMA calculates the fuel reserve as the amount of fuel required to stay aloft for that amount of time.

Table A.4. Aircraft Mission Parameters Section of KARMA Parameters File

Aircraft Mission Parameters	Mission Type	Required CAP Minutes on Station (Notional Value)	Minimum Tanker Separation Distance (nmi) (Notional Value)	Maximum Tanker Separation Distance (nmi) (Notional Value)	Fuel Reserve (lb.) (Notional Value)
Default	Default	120	0	100	1 hour flight time
F-15C	Patrol	120	240	260	2350
FA-18E	Strike	0	0	400	2146
Etc.					

NOTE: nmi = nautical mile.

KARMA Scenario-Dependent Inputs

Once the user has filled out the parameters file, the other files (the ATO file, the airfields file, the beddown file, the orbits file, and the resource damage files) must be populated. These files are stored under a scenario subfolder (e.g., Bermuda Scenario) contained in the Data folder. Thus, there will be a different version of these files for each scenario.

A STORM scenario ATO can be used as a direct input to KARMA and requires no changes. STORM is a USAF campaign model. A limitation of STORM, however, is its representation of aerial refueling. KARMA uses the non-tanker sorties in the STORM ATO to determine the fuel demand for the conflict and then calculates a tanker ATO to support the receiver ATO as well as possible.

Table A.5 provides the headers of the ATO input file that KARMA uses. Every sortie in the ATO must contain this information, but any other columns (of which there will be many in a STORM ATO file) will be ignored by KARMA.

Table A.5. ATO File

Column Heading	Type of Data or Data Options	Notional Data Example	Description
Day	Integer	3	Sortie day
AirAsset Owner	String: USAF/USN	USAF	Sorties not flown by USAF or USN will not be considered for aerial refueling or air base resources.
Mission	String: DCAP/OCAP/GDCA/GHVA/PHVA/ PSRV/SJAM/HVA or PAI/GAI/XAI/TAL/OESC/AI	DCAP	The first set of mission types maps to a patrol mission; the second set of mission types maps to a strike mission.
Planned Configuration	String	6 X AIM-120D, 2 X AIM-9M	The munitions configuration carried by the aircraft; this string needs to match a munitions configuration in munitions_configs.csv.
Target Name	String	Hamilton	The name of the target
Target Lat	Float	34.2	The latitude of the target
Target Long	Float	−65.8	The longitude of the target
AirAsset	String	F-15C	Aircraft MDS
Qty	Integer	2	Number of aircraft flying together (e.g., 2 = two-ship; 4 = four-ship)
Planned Time on Tgt	Float	1.5	Time that the aircraft must reach the target (1.5 = 12:00 p.m. on the first day of the conflict)
Status	String: Flown/Cancelled	Flown	Only flown sorties are included in calculations.
Start Location	String	Miami	Sortie takeoff location name (must match an air base in the airfields file)
Start Lat	Float	25.8	Sortie takeoff location latitude
Start Long	Float	25.8	Sortie takeoff location longitude

The airfields and beddown files must be populated separately to match the scenario. If one is using a STORM scenario, the beddown file should reflect the information (e.g., aircraft locations, squadrons) inputted into STORM. Table A.6 provides the headers of the airfields input file to KARMA. Any extra columns will be ignored. Every sortie takeoff location in the ATO must be included in the airfields file.

Table A.6. Airfields Input File

Column Heading	Type of Data or Data Options	Notional Data Example	Description
Base Name	String	3	Name of air base
Latitude	Float	25.8	Latitude of air base
Longitude	Float	25.8	Longitude of air base
Number of Runways	Integer	1	Number of runways located on air base
Runway 1 Length (ft.)[a]	Float	14,000	The length of runway 1 in feet
Temperature (F)	Float	70	The assumed temperature at takeoff
Altitude (ft.)	Integer	0	Altitude of the airfield
Total Fuel Storage (gal.)	Float	10,000,000	Total fuel storage available on base
Fuel Resupply per Day (gal.)	Float	1,000,000	The amount of fuel that gets resupplied to the air base each day; this number is used if the Take Fuel Supplies from Airfield Data Sheet parameter is set to True
Number Small Expedient Shelters	Integer	10	Number of shelters for small aircraft on air base
Number Large Aircraft Shelters	Integer	0	Number of shelters for large aircraft on air base
Takeoff Fuel Fraction	Float	1.0	This number scales the amount of fuel with which an aircraft is allowed to take off. If this number is set to 0.4, then an aircraft that usually takes off with 50,000 lb. of fuel would take off with 20,000 lb. If this fraction is set to a low value, a tanker orbit will have to be placed close to the air base so that aircraft can refuel soon after takeoff.

[a] The airfields file can contain as many runways as needed. Add columns Runway 2 Length (ft), Runway 3 Length (ft), and so on.

Table A.7 provides the headers of the beddown input file to KARMA. For this input file, column order *matters* and must be kept in the order listed in Table A.7. If there is not a sufficient number of aircraft (of a given MDS) at an air base on a day a sortie of that MDS is scheduled to take off (from that air base), the sortie will be scrubbed because of insufficient aircraft. Aircraft can move around but can be at only one place at one time. In Table A.7, there are 30 F-15Cs (they make up a squadron called Miami_F-15C) at the Miami air base on day 3. On day 4, they could move to the Chicago air base, which would be denoted by a row with values Day = 4, Base = Chicago, Aircraft = F-15C, Squadron = Miami_F-15C, and Number = 30.

Table A.7. Beddown Input File

Column Heading	Type of Data or Data Options	Notional Data Example	Description
Day	Integer	3	Conflict day
Base	String	Miami	Name of air base at which the aircraft are located on that day
Aircraft	String	F-15C	Aircraft MDS
Squadron	String	Miami_F-15C	Squadron to which the aircraft belong
Number	Integer	30	The number of that type of MDS in the squadron

NOTE: For this input file, column order *matters* and must be kept in the order listed.

Table A.8 provides the headers of the orbit input file to KARMA. This is the input file that allows analysts to move tanker orbits around (which could depend on tanker survivability assumptions, as discussed before) or decrease or increase the number of orbits.

Table A.8. Orbit Input File

Column Heading	Type of Data or Data Options	Notional Data Example	Description
Orbit Name	String	Franklin	Orbit name
Lat	Float	34.658963	Orbit latitude
Long	Float	−71.825098	Orbit longitude

Tables A.9 through A.11 provide the headers of the aircraft damage, fuel damage and resupply, and runway availability input files to KARMA. These files allow analysts to experiment with damage to these three key resources on different air bases throughout the course of the conflict. They can be created from scratch, or they can be automatically generated from TAB-VAM results.

Table A.9. Aircraft Damage Input File

Column Heading	Type of Data or Data Options	Notional Data Example	Description
Case	String	Baseline-US	Name of case for all input parameters that go into calculating air base damage
Allocation	String	Cruise-missiles-against-fuel	Combination of threat vectors that caused damage
Hour	Float	55	Hour of conflict at which damage occurred
Location	String	Chicago	Name of air base that had aircraft damage
Ramp Coverage	Float	0.42	Percentage of parking area that was damaged; translates to the percentage of aircraft parked at time of attack being destroyed
Expeditionary Small Shelter	Float	2	Number of small aircraft shelters destroyed; can be fractional
Large Shelter	Float	0	Number of large aircraft shelters destroyed; can be fractional

Table A.10. Fuel Damage and Resupply Input File

Column Heading	Type of Data or Data Options	Notional Data Example	Description
Case	String	Baseline-US	Name of case for all input parameters that go into calculating air base damage
Allocation	String	Cruise-missiles-against-fuel	Combination of threat vectors that caused damage
Hour	Float	55	Hour of conflict at which damage occurred
Location	String	Chicago	Name of air base that had aircraft damage
Fuel Destroyed (gal.)	Integer	320,000	Gallons of fuel destroyed on the air base from attack at the hour specified in the Hour parameter
Fuel Supplied (gal.)	Integer	1,000,000	The amount of fuel that gets resupplied to the air base each day; this number is used if the Take Fuel Supplies from VAM parameter is set to True

Table A.11. Runway Availability Input File

Column Heading	Type of Data or Data Options	Notional Data Example	Description
Case	String	Baseline-US	Name of case for all input parameters that go into calculating air base damage
Allocation	String	Cruise-missiles-against-fuel	Combination of threat vectors that caused damage
Hour	Float	55	Hour of conflict at which damage occurred
Location	String	Chicago	Name of air base that had aircraft damage
Aircraft Size	String: LARGE/SMALL	LARGE	For a runway attack at the hour specified in the Hour parameter, the number of hours that runways are closed depends on whether the aircraft trying to take off is large or small, because, as runways are repaired, they become functional to small aircraft faster than to large aircraft.
Hours Closed	Float	12	From the hour specified in the Hour parameter, the runway is closed to aircraft of the size specified in the Aircraft Size parameter for some number of hours (in this notional case, 12 large aircraft).

KARMA Scenario-Independent Inputs

Aircraft and munitions data files are kept in their own separate subfolders of the Data folder and are not kept in scenario subfolders because these technical specifications are not expected to change from scenario to scenario. The user may, of course, edit these data files at their discretion. New data files can be added to account for new aircraft versions or new munitions. The next set of tables explains the structure of these files so that new information can be added accordingly.

Note that the munitions configuration file translates a list of munitions package names for KARMA—e.g., the package name "4 X AIM-120F, 2X JASSM-ER" is listed along with the information that this package contains four AIM-120F munitions and two Joint Air-to-Surface Standoff Missile–Extended Range (JASSM-ER) munitions. KARMA looks up munitions package names in this list rather than attempting to parse the natural language of the package description. Because many munitions configurations are conceivable and could be named in many different ways, in practice, the user may need to update this dictionary frequently to handle a new ATO with new munitions configurations.

Aircraft Data Subfolder

Each aircraft MDS has its own data file. Table A.12 displays the contents of a generic receiver aircraft data file.[31] For example, aircraft data files contain blocks of performance data for different flight modes at different operating altitudes—e.g., "Maximum Range Cruise at Altitude 25,000 [ft]," "Maximum Range Cruise at Altitude 30,000 [ft]," "Maximum Endurance at Altitude 25,000 [ft]," "Long Range Cruise at Altitude 35,000 [ft]," "Aerial Refueling at Altitude 20,000 [ft]." An aircraft data file could contain many different flight modes at many different altitudes, or it might only contain data for a single flight mode at one altitude if other data were not available. The currently existing KARMA aircraft data files were in many cases populated by information from the 2013 version of Combat Flight Planning Software (CFPS). However, CFPS is not always consistent about which flight modes are described for each aircraft. Also, some MDS were not present in CFPS at all and had to be described based on other sources.

Table A.12. Receiver Aircraft Data File

Row Label	Type of Data or Data Options	Notional Data Example	Description
{null}	String	F-22A	Name of aircraft
Empty Weight	Integer	44,100	Weight of airframe and avionics in lb.
Internal Fuel Capacity	Integer	19,000	Internal fuel capacity in lb.
Internal Takeoff Fuel	Integer	19,000	Internal takeoff fuel in lb.
External Fuel Tank Capacity	Integer	6,000	Some aircraft carry external fuel tank(s), which gives them extra fuel capacity (in lb.).
External Fuel Tank Empty Weight	Integer	600	The weight of external fuel tank(s) in lb.
Default Cruise Speed (knots)	Integer	460	Fuel expenditure calculations are done using performance data (described later in this table), if available; if performance data are unavailable, a single value for cruise speed is used.
Default Cruise Altitude (ft.)	Integer	25,000	The default cruise altitude informs KARMA which set of performance data to use.
Aerial Refuelable?	Binary: TRUE/FALSE	TRUE	If the MDS can be aerially refueled, set to true; otherwise, set to false.

---

[31] The data in Table A.12 are completely notional, although they are of the right orders of magnitude so as to not be confusing.

Row Label	Type of Data or Data Options	Notional Data Example	Description
Refueling Intake Method	String: Boom/Drogue/None	Boom	If the MSD is aerially refueled by a boom, set to Boom; if it is aerially refueled by a drogue, set to Drogue; if it cannot be aerially refueled, set to None.
Fuel Onload Rate (lb./min.)	Integer value or string	3,000	If the aircraft fuel-onload rate is known to vary with fuel load, this parameter can be set to Variable and the Instantaneous Onload Rate supplied below. If this detailed data is not available, a constant fuel-onload rate can be specified here—e.g., 3,000 lb./min.
Ground Time (hr.)	Float	4.25	The turnaround time of the MDS
Minimum Runway Length	Integer	7,000	The minimum runway length, in feet, required for MDS to take off
Maximum Range Cruise at Altitude[a]	Integer	25,000	The following performance data are for maximum range cruise at the given altitude in feet.
Total Aircraft Weight	List of integers	63,407, 62,683, 59,429, 56,264	A list of aircraft weights in lb.
Speed (knots)	List of integers	484, 480, 474, 468	List of aircraft speeds corresponding with weights (e.g., for maximum range cruise at the given altitude, the aircraft should cruise at 480 knots when aircraft weight is between 63,407 and 62,683 lb.)
Fuel Consumed Per Hour	List of floats	6,696, 6,352, 6,112, 6,093	List of fuel-burn rates corresponding with weights (e.g., fuel-burn rate is 6,352 lb./hr. when aircraft weight is between 63,407 and 62,683 lb.)
Specific Range (nmi/lb.)	List of floats	0.084, 0.085, 0.087, 0.090	List of specific ranges corresponding with weights (e.g., specific range is 0.085 nmi/lb. when aircraft weight is between 63,407 and 62,683 lb.)
Maximum Endurance at Altitude[b]	Integer	25,000	The following performance data are for maximum endurance at the given altitude in feet.
Total Aircraft Weight	List of integers	61,653, 58,383	A list of aircraft weights
Speed (knots)	List of integers	508, 509	List of aircraft speeds corresponding with weights (e.g., for maximum endurance at the given altitude, the aircraft should cruise at 508 knots when aircraft weight is between 61,653 and 58,383 lb.)
Fuel Consumed Per Hour	List of floats	6,540, 6,260	List of fuel-burn rates corresponding with weights (e.g., fuel-burn rate is 6,260 lb./hr.

Row Label	Type of Data or Data Options	Notional Data Example	Description
			when aircraft weight is between 61,653 and 58,383 lb.)
Specific Range (nmi/lb.)	List of floats	0.078, 0.081	List of specific ranges corresponding with weights (e.g., specific range is 0.081 nmi/lb. when aircraft weight is between 61,653 and 58,383 lb.)
{null}	String	Variable Fuel Onload Rate[c]	Prefaces variable fuel-onload data
Current Fuel Load (lb.)	List of floats	5,000, 10,000 14,000 18,000	List of current fuel loads
Instantaneous Onload Rate (lb./min.)	List of floats	3,900 3,650 3,640 960	Corresponding list of instantaneous onload rates (e.g., with 5,000 lb. of fuel, this notional F-22A could take on 3,900 lb. of fuel in 1 minute)
Average Flow Rate to Full Tanks (lb./min.)	List of floats	3,100 2,700 1,280 550	Corresponding list of average flow rates to fill tank (e.g., with 5,000 lb. of fuel, this notional F-22A would require an average of 3,100 lb. of fuel per minute to fill up)

[a] The performance data for maximum range cruise flying at the specified altitude exist as a block of information. The performance data must come after the line that sets the maximum range cruise altitude. Additional blocks of performance data can be added for different maximum range cruise altitudes.

[b] The performance data for maximum endurance flying is also a block of information that must follow the line setting the maximum endurance altitude. Additional blocks of performance data can be added for different altitudes of maximum endurance flight.

[c] This is not a notional value. This line signifies that the next three lines of data provide variable fuel-ionload performance data.

NOTE: When the unit (e.g., ft. or lb.) is not explicitly a part of the input parameter, it is included in the description for clarity. In the future, these parameters can be renamed to explicitly include units.

Tanker aircraft have a few additional pieces of information in their respective data files. Table A.13 lists these extra data.

Row Label	Type of Data or Data Options	Notional Data Example	Description
Reconfigurable in Flight	Binary: TRUE/FALSE	TRUE	If the tanker can switch between boom and drogue refueling midflight, set to true; otherwise, set to false.
Max Drogue Nozzles	Integer	1	The maximum number of drogue lines on the tanker
Max Boom Nozzles	Integer	1	The maximum number of booms on the tanker
Aerial Refueling at Altitude[a]	Integer	30,000	Altitude for aerial refueling performance data described below
Total Aircraft Weight	List of integers	300,000, 280,000, 260,000, 240,000	A list of tanker weights
Speed (knots)	List of integers	370, 390, 410, 420	List of aircraft speeds correlating with weights (e.g., 370 knots corresponds to a 300,000-lb. tanker)
Fuel Consumed Per Hour	List of floats	20,000, 15,000, 14,300, 13,200	List of fuel burns correlating with weights (e.g., 20,000 lb./hr. corresponds to a 300,000-lb. tanker)
Specific Range (nmi/lb.)	List of floats	0.02, 0.03, 0.04, 0.045	List of specific ranges correlating with weights (e.g., 0.02 nmi/lb. corresponds to a 300,000-lb. tanker)

[a] The performance data for aerial refueling flying are also a block of information that must follow the line setting the maximum aerial refueling altitude.

Munitions Data Subfolder

The Munitions Data subfolder contains a table (munitions_weights.csv) that is a list of possible munitions and their weights in pounds. Table A.14 illustrates the munitions weight table.

Table A.14. Munitions Weights Data File

Column Heading	Type of Data or Data Options	Notional Data Example	Description
Primary Name	String	AIM-120	The name of the munition, as written in the munitions configuration
Weight (lb.)	Integer	335	The weight of the munition in lb.[a]

[a] The user specifies the munitions configuration of each receiver mission. A munitions configuration may include external fuel tanks. FUEL TANK is thus included in the munitions configuration, but its weight is left unspecified ("Depends" in the data file). The weight of an external fuel tank is actually set in the aircraft data file of the aircraft carrying the extra fuel (not in the munitions weights data file).

Table A.15 provides the headers of the munitions configuration (munitions_configs.csv) input file to KARMA, also stored in the Munitions Data subfolder within the top-level Data folder. As described before, it is essentially a dictionary that informs the program which munitions make up each munitions configuration package. The name of the configuration and the number of each munitions that make up the configuration are denoted.

Table A.15. Munitions Configuration Input File

Column Heading	Type of Data or Data Options	Notional Data Example	Description
Configuration	String	4 X AIM-120F, 2 X JASSM-ER	Name of the configuration (we recommend that it be descriptive) that matches planned munitions configurations in the ATO
AIM-120D	Integer	0	Number of AIM-120Ds in the configuration
AIM-120C	Integer	0	Number of AIM-120Cs in the configuration
AIM-120F	Integer	4	Number of AIM-120Fs in the configuration
AIM-9X	Integer	0	Number of AIM-9Xs in the configuration
JASSM	Integer	0	Number of JASSMs in the configuration
JASSM-ER	Integer	2	Number of JASSM-ERs in the configuration
Etc.[a]			

[a] The number of columns in the munitions configuration file depends on the number and variety of configurations. There has to be a column for each type of munition contained by all of the listed configurations. A few representative munitions and how they would be marked for the notional configuration (4 X AIM-120F, 2 X JASSM-ER) are shown in Table A.7.
NOTE: JASSM = Joint Air-to-Surface Standoff Missile.

Appendix B. Output Files

After the final tanker ATO has been calculated, the activity of the receiver and tanker fleets is recorded in several output files. We review these files in this appendix. Note that the Comment columns in output files are automatically generated by KARMA.

Receiver Mission History Output File

The Receiver Mission History.csv output file contains the details of all non-tanker missions, including receiver missions that do not require tanker support. Table B.1 shows a notional two-ship F-22 mission as it would be depicted in the file. Every stage of the mission, from takeoff, to how long the receivers spend aerially refueling, to which tanker tails do the fuel transfers, is accounted for. The Time column contains the day (e.g., 001) followed by the time (e.g., 03:38), separated by a slash. AC0 and AC1 stand for aircraft 0 and aircraft 1, each representing one of the two F-22s in the two-ship mission.

Table B.1. Notional Receiver Mission Histories

Mission 004	F-22A	x2							
Time	Location	ACO Fuel Remaining (minutes)	AC1 Fuel Remaining (minutes)	Total Distance Traveled	Total Time Elapsed	Average Speed (knots)	Mission Stage	Comment	
001/03:38	DC	162	162	0	000/00:00	0	0	Ready for take-off	
001/05:17	224 Teddy	44.3	44.3	817.87	000/01:39	492.5	1	Tanker Mission 64 (KC-135) refueled 2 aircraft in 6.4 + 6.6 = 13.0 minutes	
001/05:30	224 Teddy	155.6	162	817.87	000/01:52	435.69	2	Refueling 2 aircraft was scheduled to take 6.4 + 6.6 = 13.0 minutes	
001/06:00	Bermuda1	121	127.3	1,058.06	000/02:21	447.40	3	Arrived at destination	
001/07:28	Bermuda1	33	39.3	1,803.54	000/03:49	470.60	4	Flew for 88.0 minutes	
001/07:57	224 Teddy	0	6.3	2,043.72	000/04:19	473.07	5	Tanker Mission 92 (KC-46A) refueled 2 aircraft in 8.0 + 8.0 = 16.0 minutes	
001/08:13	224 Teddy	154.3	162	2,043.72	000/04:35	445.55	6	Refueling 2 aircraft was scheduled to take 8.0 + 8.0 = 16.0 minutes	
001/08:13	224 Teddy	154.3	162	2,043.72	000/04:35	445.55	7	Departed 224 Teddy for DC	
001/09:52	DC	37	45.1	2,861.60	000/06:14	458.03	8	--	
001/09:52	DC	37	45.1	2,861.60	000/06:14	458.03	9	Arrived back at base	

NOTE: ACO and AC1 stand for aircraft 0 and aircraft 1, each representing one of the two F-22s in the two-ship mission.

Tanker Mission History Output File

The Tanker Mission History.csv output file contains the details of every tanker mission. Table B.2 shows an example of the various stages of a tanker mission history. We chose tanker mission 64 because it refueled receiver mission 4, detailed in Table B.1. The bingo time at each mission stage is the latest time that it can be on orbit before it must depart the orbit.[32] If the tanker were to stay on the orbit longer, it would not be able to return to its home base without dipping into its fuel reserve, which is strictly not allowed. There is another output file called Tanker Tail History.csv, which has exactly the same information for each mission, but the information is coupled by tanker tail. For example, in this simulation of our notional Bermuda scenario, tanker mission 64 is executed by tanker tail 764. Tanker tail 764 also executes mission 193, and the information about mission 193 is listed below that of 064.

Table B.2. Notional Tanker Mission 64 History

Tanker 064	KC-135	x1			
Time	Location	Fuel Remaining (lb.)	Bingo Time	Mission Stage	Comment
001/02:19	Chicago	190,000	000/00:00	0	Takeoff
001/05:17	224 Teddy	148,991	001/15:34	1	Arrived to support Mission 4 (F-22A x2)
001/05:30	224 Teddy	118,928	001/12:37	2	Refueled Mission 4 (F-22A x2) in 6.4 + 6.6 = 13.0 minutes
001/06:49	224 Teddy	69,673	001/08:45	3	Refueled Mission 27 (F-35A x2) in 13.1 + 13.2 = 26.3 minutes
001/06:49	224 Teddy	69,673	001/08:45	4	Departed 224 Teddy for Chicago
001/10:08	Chicago	37,036	001/08:45	5	Arrived back at base

Tanker Orbit Schedules

The tanker orbit schedules are output in the Stop Schedules.csv file. Each orbit has a long list of tankers and receivers that arrive to provide and receive fuel. In Table B.3, we show a snippet of the notional tanker orbit Teddy's schedule that receiver mission 4 visits. There is significant overlap of information between the stop schedule and receiver mission history files; however, they are generated from different data structures. Cross-referencing the two is a good way of catching any problems that may arise in the simulation.

---

[32] It does not have a bingo time at takeoff because it has not yet left its home base.

Table B.3. Notional Snippet of Tanker Orbit 224 Teddy Stop Schedule

Stop 224 Teddy									
Mission	Number of Aircraft	Type of Aircraft	Refueling Type Required	Location	Altitude (x100)	Begin Refueling Time	End Refueling Time	Offload (x1,000 lb.)	Comment
64	1	KC-135	Boom	224 Teddy	200	001/05:17	001/05:17	0	Arrived to support Mission 4 (F-22A x2)
4	2	F-22A	Boom	224 Teddy	200	001/05:17	001/05:30	27	Tanker Mission 64 (KC-135) refueled 2 aircraft in 6.4 + 6.6 = 13.0 minutes
64	1	KC-135	Boom	224 Teddy	200	001/05:17	001/05:30	−27	Refueled Mission 4 (F-22A x2) in 6.4 + 6.6 = 13.0 minutes

Modified ATO Output File

Another important output file is the modified version of the original ATO. In addition to the column headings in the original ATO file, we have appended information about each sortie. This is summarized in Table B.4.

47

Table B.4. Additional Information Appended to the Receiver ATO

Column Heading	Type of Data or Output Options	Notional Data Example	Description
This Mission Modeled?	Binary: TRUE/FALSE	TRUE	This column states whether the mission was modeled by KARMA. A mission in the original STORM ATO might not be modeled by KARMA, for example, if KARMA had no information on the aircraft type.
Outcome (flown/scrubbed)	String: Flown/Scrubbed	Flown	Missions that can be supported are marked Flown. Missions canceled because resources were not available are marked Scrubbed.
Final Tanker Orbit Name	String	224 Teddy	Name of the final tanker orbit near the CAP or Strike location at which the receiver is aerially refueled
Final Tanker Orbit Latitude	Float	35.671	Latitude of the final tanker
Final Tanker Orbit Longitude	Float	−70.339	Longitude of the final tanker
Distance from Tanker to Destination (nmi)	Float	150.4	Distance from the final tanker orbit to the target location
Total Distance Traveled (nmi)	Integer	2,862	Total distance the receiver aircraft flew during the mission
T1 (minutes transit from takeoff to final tanker or station)	Integer	100	Time in minutes required for the receiver aircraft to fly from home base to the final tanker (or to the final destination, if there was no tanker)
T2 (minutes on station)	Integer	120	Time in minutes that the receiver spent on station
T3 (minutes transit around station)	Integer	80	Time in minutes of mission duration *other than* that accounted for by T1, T2, and T4. If non-zero, this is the accumulated time the receiver spends traveling back and forth between its final tanker and final station.
T4 (minutes transit returning to base)	Integer	100	Time in minutes required for the receiver aircraft to fly back to base from the final tanker (or from the final destination if there was no tanker)
Outbound Refuelings	Integer	1	The number of aerial refueling stops the receivers made going to their destination
On-Station Refuelings	Integer	3	The number of aerial refueling trips the receivers made while on station
Homebound Refuelings	Integer	1	The number of aerial refueling stops the receivers made going back to their home base
Total Fuel Burned (lb.)	Integer	98,915	The total amount of fuel that the receivers burned throughout their mission

48

Column Heading	Type of Data or Output Options	Notional Data Example	Description
Scrub Reason	String	N/A	If the mission flew, then the scrub reason is not available. If the mission was scrubbed, then a reason is given.
Squadron	String	Miami_F-22A_1	The name of the squadron to which the aircraft tails that flew the mission belong
Tail 0	Integer	602	The tail number of the first receiver in the n-ship mission (in this case, a two-ship mission)
Tail 1	Integer	603	The tail number of the second receiver in the n-ship mission (in this case, a two-ship mission)
. . . Tail n	Integer	--	Each tail number is provided up to the number of tails in the n-ship mission

Tanker ATO Output File

The last important output file is tanker ATO. The data in this file are summarized in Table B.5.

Table B.5. Receiver ATO Output File

Column Heading	Type of Data or Output Options	Notional Data Example	Description
Tanker Mission Number	Integer	64	The tanker mission number
Orbit Name	String	224 Teddy	The name of the orbit at which the tanker mission did its refueling
Orbit Latitude	Float	35.67	The latitude of the tanker orbit
Orbit Longitude	Float	−70.34	The longitude of the tanker orbit
Air Asset Type	String	KC-135	The type of tanker that executed the mission
Takeoff Time	String	001/02:19	The day and time the mission starts
Start Location	String	Chicago	The home base of the tanker at the day of takeoff
Start Latitude	String	41.8	The latitude of the home base
Start Longitude	String	−97.6	The longitude of the home base
Total Sortie Duration	Float	468.29	The total number of minutes of the tanker mission
Minutes Transit to Orbit	Float	177.9	The number of minutes spent flying between the home base and the tanker orbit
Minutes on Station	Float	91.9	The number of minutes the tanker spent at orbit
Minutes Transit Back to Base	Float	198.5	The number of minutes the tanker spent flying back from the orbit to home base
Total Fuel Burned	Float	81,972.5	The total amount of fuel the tanker burned during the mission
Total Fuel Offload	Float	62,179.1	The total amount of fuel the tanker transferred during the mission
Total Distance Traveled	Float	3,524.1	The total distance the tanker flew during the mission
Distance to Orbit	Float	1,322.4	The distance the tanker flew between its home base and orbit
Squadron	String	Chicago_KC-135_1	The name of the squadron to which the tanker tail that executed the mission belongs
Tail 0	Integer	764	The tanker tail that executed the mission

Bibliography

Barnes, J. Wesley, Victor D. Wiley, James T. Moore, and David M. Ryer, "Solving the Aerial Fleet Refueling Problem Using Group Theoretic Tabu Search," *Mathematical and Computer Modelling*, Vol. 39, No. 6-8, 2004, pp. 617–640.

Bickel, William G., Jr., *Improving the Analysis Capabilities of the Synthetic Theater Operations Research Model (STORM)*, Monterey, Calif.: Naval Postgraduate School, September 2014.

Bolkom, Christopher, *Air Force Aerial Refueling Methods: Flying Boom Versus Hose-and-Drogue*, Congressional Research Service Report RL32910, June 5, 2006.

Emerson, Donald E., *An Introduction to the TSAR Simulation Program: Model Features and Logic,* Santa Monica, Calif.: RAND Corporation, R-2584-AF, 1982. As of September 27, 2018:
https://www.rand.org/pubs/reports/R2584.html

Gormley, Dennis M., *Dealing with the Threat of Cruise Missiles*, Abingdon, UK: Routledge, 2013.

Hackler, George C., *Goal Programming Tanker Beddown Decisions*, Wright-Patterson Air Force Base, Ohio: Air Force Institute of Technology, graduate research project, AFIT/ILM/ENS/08-03, June 2008.

Hagen, Jeff, Bradley DeBlois, James S. Chow, Alexander C. Hou, Fred Timson, and James Williams, *Assessing Survivability Options for Air Refueling Tankers*, Santa Monica, Calif.: RAND Corporation, forthcoming, not available to the general public.

Insinna, Valerie, "KC-Y Competition Still Under Consideration as Air Force Works to Define Future Tanker Fleet," *Defense News*, November 29, 2016.

Jackson, Jack, *Mobility Capabilities and Requirements Study 2016 Accreditation Report*, Vol. 1, Institute for Defense Analyses, IDA Paper P-4475, July 2009.

Lostumbo, Michael, Michael J. McNerney, Eric Peltz, Derek Eaton, David R. Frelinger, Victoria Greenfield, John Halliday, Patrick Mills, Bruce R. Nardulli, Stacie L. Pettyjohn, Jerry M. Sollinger, and Stephen M. Worman, *Overseas Basing of U.S. Military Forces: An Assessment of Relative Costs and Strategic Benefits*, Santa Monica, Calif.: RAND

Corporation, RR-201-OSD, 2013. As of September 27, 2018:
https://www.rand.org/pubs/research_reports/RR201.html

McCoy, Allen, *Modeling Aerial Refueling Operations*, St. Louis, Mo.: Washington University in St. Louis, doctoral thesis, January 2010.

Orletsky, David T., Michael Kennedy, Bradley DeBlois, Daniel M. Norton, Richard Mason, Dahlia Anne Goldfeld, Andrew Karode, Jeff Hagen, James S. Chow, James Williams, Alexander C. Hou, and Michael J. Lostumbo, *Options to Enhance Air Mobility in Anti-Access/Area Denial Environments*, Santa Monica, Calif.: RAND Corporation, forthcoming, not available to the general public.

Panos, Dennis C., *Approximate Dynamic Programming and Aerial Refueling*, Princeton, N.J.: Princeton University, master's thesis, June 2007.

Romano, Daniel M., Rachel Costello, Bradley DeBlois, Robert A. Guffey, Andrew Karode, Christopher Lynch, Ricardo Sanchez, Alexander Stephenson, Devin Tierney, Brent Thomas, and Robert S. Tripp, *Passive and Active Defense Postures to Support Joint/Allied Combat Operations in Denied Environments Against Missile Attacks*, Santa Monica, Calif.: RAND Corporation, 2016, not available to the general public.

SciPy, "Optimization (scipy.optimize)," *SciPy v.1.0.0 Reference Guide*, October 25, 2017. As of September 27, 2018:
https://docs.scipy.org/doc/scipy/reference/tutorial/optimize.html

Seymour, Christian N., *Capturing the Full Potential of the Synthetic Theater Operations Research Model (STORM)*, Monterey, Calif.: Naval Postgraduate School, September 2014.

Stevens, Donald, David Ochmanek, and Lowell H. Schwartz, *Power Projection in an "Anti-Access" Environment: Implications for USAF Modernization*, Santa Monica, Calif.: RAND Corporation, 2007, not available to the general public.

Stillion, John, and David A. Orletsky, *Airbase Vulnerability to Conventional Cruise-Missile and Ballistic-Missile Attacks: Technology, Scenarios, and U.S. Air Force Responses*, Santa Monica, Calif.: RAND Corporation, MR-1028-AF, 1999. As of September 27, 2018:
https://www.rand.org/pubs/monograph_reports/MR1028.html

Thomas, Brent, Mahyar A. Amouzegar, Rachel Costello, Robert A. Guffey, Andrew Karode, Christopher Lynch, Kristin F. Lynch, Ken Munson, Chad J. R. Ohlandt, Daniel M. Romano, Ricardo Sanchez, Robert S. Tripp, and Joseph Vesely, *Project AIR FORCE Modeling*

Capabilities for Support of Combat Operations in Denied Environments, Santa Monica, Calif.: RAND Corporation, RR-427-AF, 2015. As of September 27, 2018: https://www.rand.org/pubs/research_reports/RR427.html

Tripp, Robert S., Brent Thomas, Rachel Costello, Robert A. Guffey, Andrew Karode, and Christopher Lynch, *Combat Operations in Denied Environments: Evolving Strategies for Ensuring Air Force Resilience in the Pacific Theater*, Santa Monica, Calif.: RAND Corporation, 2015, not available to the general public.

U.S. Air Force, *KC-46A Pegasus*, fact sheet, February 1, 2016.